RECONSTRUCTION IN THE SOUTH

Problems in American Civilization

UNDER THE EDITORIAL DIRECTION OF

George Rogers Taylor

RECONSTRUCTION
in the SOUTH

EDITED WITH AN INTRODUCTION BY
Edwin C. Rozwenc

Problems in American Civilization

READINGS SELECTED BY THE
DEPARTMENT OF AMERICAN STUDIES
AMHERST COLLEGE

D. C. HEATH AND COMPANY: Boston

INTRODUCTION

THE English historian, Herbert Butterfield, in examining the "psychology of historians," discovered a "passionate desire to come to a judgment of values, to make history answer questions and decide issues and to give the historian the last word in a controversy." Moved by this desire, the historian "imagines that he is inconclusive unless he can give a verdict . . . he feels that loose threads are still left hanging unless he can show which party was in the right." It was in response to this deep desire that history "has been taken out of the hands of the strolling minstrels and the pedlars of stories and has been accepted as a means by which we can gain more understanding of ourselves and our place in the sun — a more clear consciousness of what we are tending to and what we are trying to do."[1]

The Reconstruction of the South after the Civil War ushered in one of those periods of political and social struggle which make a necessity and a virtue of the besetting desire of the historian to make history answer questions and decide issues. For this was a critical conjuncture in the history of the United States. After four years of bloody civil war, the victorious North faced the problem of restoring or recreating a union of states which had been disrupted by secession. It was indeed a task "fraught with great difficulty," as President Lincoln warned in his last public address, the more so, as he was quick to point out, because "we, the loyal people, differ among ourselves as to the mode, manner and measures of reconstruction." Out of those differences, and many more besides, came the bitter controversies of the Reconstruction period and the historian, no less than Lincoln and his contemporaries and successors, must make decisions and come to a judgment of values about that era if he is to give his reader a meaningful story of the American experience.

Nevertheless, among the first to express full judgments in literature about the workings of Reconstruction in the South were "strolling minstrels" and "pedlars of stories" rather than historians. In the South, Sidney Lanier relieved his feelings of indignation over Reconstruction policies with several poems of protest. In an uncollected poem in dialect, "Civil Rights" (1874), Lanier denounced the cruel purpose of Yankee civil rights legislation.

Hit seems as ef, just when the water's roughest
    here of late,
Them Yanks had throwed us overboard from off
    the Ship of State.
Yes, throwed us both — both black and white —
    into the ragin' sea,
Without but one rotten plank; while they, all safe
    and free,
Stands on the decks, and rams their hands into
    their pocket tight,
And laughs to see we both must drown, or live
    by makin' fight![2]

[1] *The Whig Interpretation of History* (London: G. Bell & Sons, 1950), pp. 64–65.

[2] As quoted in Aubrey Harrison Starke, *Sidney Lanier* (Chapel Hill: University of North Carolina Press, 1933), p. 187.

In an equally critical vein, Joel Chandler Harris not only attacked the abuses of Reconstruction in editorials and essays, but also wrote a rather negligible novel in a Reconstruction setting, *Gabriel Tolliver,* in which the Freedmen's Bureau and Union League were pictured as sinister agents in the life of the South.

On the northern side, the Ohio-born Union army officer, Albion W. Tourgée, wrote with equal intensity such novels as *A Fool's Errand* (1879) and *Bricks without Straw* (1880). In these he deplored the failure of the North to follow through with policies which would have made the civil and political rights of the Negro secure in the face of the persisting pattern of political oligarchy and inculcated race fear in southern life. Although *A Fool's Errand* was hailed by dozens of northern newspapers as the *Uncle Tom's Cabin* of the Reconstruction period, both the book and the author have been forgotten by students of American history and literature. Nevertheless, Tourgée's novels reveal much of the mind and temper of the radical Republican idealist in the Reconstruction period.

While poets and novelists expressed themselves so immediately about the issues of southern Reconstruction, there was not much significant historical writing about Reconstruction until the opening decade of the twentieth century. The sectional apologetics which were written in the immediate post-Civil War decade were concerned with the Civil War itself and the questions of secession and slavery connected with that struggle. To be sure, Jefferson Davis in his *The Rise and Fall of the Confederate Government,* Alexander Stephens in the *War between the States,* and Edward Pollard in *The Lost Cause* wrote bitter concluding chapters about the "final subjugation" of the southern states, but these were mere addenda to their main task of justifying the Confederacy. On the other side, Henry Wilson in his chapters on Reconstruction, in the *History of the Rise and Fall of the Slave Power in America,* almost never gets outside of the Senate chamber, where he played a minor role. Horace Greeley avoided the subject completely in his *American Conflict.*

Not until James Ford Rhodes wrote his volumes on the history of the United States did a considerable body of scholarly historical writing on Reconstruction appear. Rhodes, in the two volumes he devoted to the political history of the Reconstruction period, took the position that the radical Reconstruction program had prevented a happy readjustment of the South to the Union. In his opinion, the evils that he pictured in the South came from the forcing of universal Negro suffrage upon the South — an action which he described as the "worst provision" of the Reconstruction Acts. James Schouler, who completed his voluminous *History of the United States under the Constitution* with a volume on the Reconstruction period, concurred fully with Rhodes' opinion on the evil effects of Reconstruction policies upon the South. The general political histories of Rhodes and Schouler were supported by the monographic studies of individual southern states guided and influenced by William Archibald Dunning in his seminar at Columbia University. These scholarly studies, together with Dunning's own writings on the subject, produced an impressive body of historical writing which exposed the corruption and abuses of government in the South under carpetbagger and Negro domination and dealt sympathetically with the efforts of those who worked to restore white supremacy to the South. A similar view was taken by other academic historians of the period — Walter Fleming, John W. Burgess, and Woodrow Wilson. As a matter of fact, a striking degree of acquiescence in the interpretations of Rhodes and Dunning characterized the writing and teaching of American historians in the years that followed and, to a considerable degree, those interpretations are still held widely by American historians.

More recently, however, there has been a tendency to revise the interpretations of the Rhodes and Dunning generation by examining more closely some of the social and economic changes that came in the South during the Reconstruction period and by re-examining the motivations of conflicting political groups in the South — Negroes, carpetbaggers, scalawags, white restorationists — in the more objective way of the political scientist who seeks to probe the purposes, slogans, and the power potentialities of interest groups. The writings of these historians suggest that there were many constructive social and political developments in the Reconstruction period and assert that honesty and dishonesty in politics were not monopolies of any one group.

The readings in this volume are designed to give the reader varying samples of interpretative historical writing about the Reconstruction of the South. The first selection is an eassay written by Woodrow Wilson, one of an interesting series of articles on Reconstruction which appeared in the *Atlantic Monthly* at the turn of our own century. This selection not only reflects the interpretation of the Rhodes and Dunning generation but also provides a compact review of the political and constitutional measures of the Radical Republican reconstruction program. The selection from Professor Randall's widely used book *Civil War and Reconstruction* is a modern portrayal of the effects of Reconstruction in the South which is still strongly influenced by the tradition established by Rhodes, Dunning, and Schouler.

The next five selections are designed to give the reader a closer look at particular southern states. The chapter from Roger Shugg's study of classes and politics in Louisiana is an interesting example of the new methods of historical analysis followed by the younger generation of historians which, however, does not in any sense diminish the importance of corruption in Louisiana during the turbulent days of Reconstruction. The chapter from Walter Fleming's classic study of Reconstruction in Alabama should be compared with the more recent article by Horace Mann Bond, who attempted to get at "underlying" social and economic forces in Alabama. The selection from Wharton's study of the Negro in Mississippi represents one of the most careful attempts to measure the actual degree of Negro participation in politics and officeholding. And finally in this group is a chapter on Reconstruction in South Carolina written with intensity of racial feeling as well as with a Marxist frame of reference by the Negro historian, William Burghardt Du Bois.

The last two selections are in the nature of a summing up of the argument. The article by Professor Simkins is an attempt to justify what might be called a modern "revisionist" interpretation of the Reconstruction period. The chapter from Professor Coulter's recent book on Reconstruction in the notable *History of the South* series represents a conscious rejection by a present-day historian of the attempt to establish a "revisionist" interpretation of Reconstruction in the South.

The reader will have to determine for himself whether the Reconstruction of the

South must be judged to have been primarily a "blackout of honest government" resulting from political rule by ignorant Negroes and villainous white carpetbaggers and scalawags, or whether the story of Reconstruction should be written in terms of "quietly constructive" political and social achievements which are not adequately reflected by the "abnormalities of post-bellum politics." But as Herbert Butterfield reminds us, we must be sure that our judgments, whatever they may be, shall adequately take account of all of the complexities in the intricate processes at work in any historical period.

CONTENTS

CONTENTS

THE CLASH OF ISSUES

A leading political scientist and historian wrote at the opening of our century:

"It was the most soul-sickening spectacle that America had ever been called upon to behold. Every principle of the old American polity was here reversed. In place of government by the most intelligent and virtuous part of the people for the benefit of the governed, here was government by the most ignorant and vicious part of the population for the benefit, the vulgar, materialistic, brutal benefit of the governing set."

— JOHN W. BURGESS

The author of a standard modern textbook on Civil War and Reconstruction echoes this view, in part, when he asserts:

"To use a modern phrase, government under Radical Republican rule in the South had become a kind of 'racket.'"

—J. G. RANDALL

On the other hand, a distinguished Negro historian declares:

"In South Carolina, Mississippi and Louisiana, the proportion of Negroes was so large, their leaders of sufficient power, and the Federal control so effective that for the years 1868–1874 the will of black labor was powerful; and so far as it was intelligently led, and had definite goals, it took perceptible steps toward public education, confiscation of large incomes, betterment of labor conditions, universal suffrage, and in some cases distribution of land to the peasant."

— W. E. BURGHARDT DU BOIS

Moreover, a southern historian of our own generation has written:

"The capital blunder of the chronicle of Reconstruction is to treat the period like Carlyle's portrayal of the French Revolution, as a melodrama involving wild-eyed conspirators whose acts are best described in red flashes upon a canvas. . . . Of course the South during Reconstruction, like France during the Revolution, had its prophets of despair, its fanatical idealists, its unprincipled knaves. Luckily the behavior of these damned souls is not the whole story of Reconstruction, but merely a partial recording of the political aspects of the era. Some of the political acts were as sane and constructive as those of the French Revolution. They were concerned with educational, constitutional, and political reform, and were instrumental in putting the southern states in line with the progressive spirit of the nineteenth century."

— FRANCIS B. SIMKINS

Nevertheless, the historian who has made the most recent comprehensive study of the South during Reconstruction insists:

"Radical Reconstruction was doomed to fail. With a crass, materialistic design, it was cloaked in a garb of high idealistic justice, but its rulers were inexperienced, ignorant and corrupt. They forgot what the world had learned and experienced during the preceding two thousand years. Milleniums and Utopias might be written about, but intelligent people knew that they were never to be realized in this life."

— E. Merton Coulter

Woodrow Wilson:

THE RECONSTRUCTION OF THE SOUTHERN STATES

. . . THE war had been fought to preserve the Union, to dislodge and drive out by force the doctrine of the right of secession. The southern states *could* not legally leave the Union — such had been the doctrine of the victorious states whose armies won under Grant and Sherman — and the federal government had been able to prevent their leaving, in fact. In strict theory, though their people had been in revolt, under organizations which called themselves states, and which had thrown off all allegiance to the older Union and formed a new confederation of their own, Virginia, North Carolina, South Carolina, Florida, Georgia, Mississippi, Alabama, Louisiana, Texas, Arkansas, and Tennessee, the historic states once solemnly embodied in the Union, had never gone out of it, could never go out of it and remain states. In fact, nevertheless, their representatives had withdrawn from the federal House and Senate; their several governments, without change of form or personnel, had declared themselves no longer joined with the rest of the states in purpose or allegiance, had arranged a new and separate partnership, and had for four years maintained an organized resistance to the armies of the Union which they had renounced. Now that their resistance had been overcome and their confederacy destroyed, how were they to be treated? As if they had been

all the while in the Union, whether they would or no, and were now at last simply brought to their senses again, to take up their old-time rights and duties intact, resume their familiar functions within the Union as if nothing had happened? The theory of the case was tolerably clear; and the Supreme Court of the United States presently supplied lawyers, if not statesmen, with a clear enough formulation of it. The Constitution, it said (for example, in the celebrated case of Texas *vs.* White, decided in 1868), had created an indestructible Union of indestructible states. The eleven states which had attempted to secede had not been destroyed by their secession. Everything that they had done to bring about secession or maintain resistance to the Union was absolutely null and void, and without legal effect; but their laws passed for other purposes, even those passed while they were in fact maintaining their resolution of secession and defying the authority of the national government, were valid, and must be given effect to in respect of all the ordinary concerns of business, property, and personal obligation, just as if they had been passed in ordinary times and under ordinary circumstances. The states had lost no legitimate authority; their acts were invalid only in respect of what they had never had the right to do.

But it was infinitely hard to translate

Woodrow Wilson, "The Reconstruction of the Southern States," *Atlantic Monthly,* LXXXVII (January, 1901), 2–11. Used by permission of the *Atlantic Monthly.*

such principles into a practicable rule of statesmanship. It was as difficult and hazardous a matter to reinstate the states as it would have been had their legal right to secede been first admitted, and then destroyed by the revolutionary force of arms. It became, whatever the theory, in fact a process of reconstruction. Had Mr. Lincoln lived, perhaps the whole of the delicate business might have been carried through with dignity, good temper, and simplicity of method; with all necessary concessions to passion, with no pedantic insistence upon consistent and uniform rules, with sensible irregularities and compromises, and yet with a straightforward, frank, and open way of management which would have assisted to find for every influence its natural and legitimate and quieting effect. It was of the nature of Mr. Lincoln's mind to reduce complex situations to their simples, to guide men without irritating them, to go forward and be practical without being radical — to serve as a genial force which supplied heat enough to keep action warm, and yet minimized the friction and eased the whole progress of affairs.

It was characteristic of him that he had kept his own theory clear and unconfused throughout the whole struggle to bring the southern people back to their allegiance to the Union. He had never recognized any man who spoke or acted for the southern people in the matter of secession as the representative of any government whatever. It was, in his view, not the southern states which had taken up arms against the Union, but merely the people dwelling within them. State lines defined the territory within which rebellion had spread and men had organized under arms to destroy the Union; but their organization had been effected without color of law; that could not be a state, in any legal meaning of the term, which denied what was the indispensable prerequisite of its every exercise of political functions, its membership in the Union. He was not fighting states, therefore, or a confederacy of states, but only a body of people who refused to act as states, and could not, if they would, form another Union. What he wished and strove for, without passion save for the accomplishment of his purpose, without enmity against persons, and yet with burning hostility against what the southerners meant to do, was to bring the people of the southern states once more to submission and allegiance; to assist them, when subdued, to rehabilitate the states whose territory and resources, whose very organization, they had used to effect a revolution; to do whatever the circumstances and his own powers, whether as President or merely as an influential man and earnest friend of peace, might render possible to put them back, defeated, but not conquered or degraded, into the old-time hierarchy of the Union.

There were difficulties and passions in the way which possibly even Mr. Lincoln could not have forced within any plan of good will and simple restoration; but he had made a hopeful beginning before he died. He had issued a proclamation of amnesty so early as 1863, offering pardon and restoration to civil rights to all who would abandon resistance to the authority of the Union, and take the oath of unreserved loyalty and submission which he prescribed; and as the war drew to an end, and he saw the power of the Union steadily prevail, now here, now there, throughout an ever increasing area, he earnestly begged that those who had taken the oath and returned to their allegiance would unite in positive and concerted action, organize their states upon the old footing, and make ready for a full restoration of the old conditions. Let those who had taken the oath, and were ready to bind themselves in all good faith to accept the acts and proclamations of the federal government in the matter of slavery — let all, in short, who were willing to accept the actual results of the war, organize themselves and set up governments made conformable to the new order of things, and he would recognize them as the people of the states within which they acted, ask Congress to admit their representatives, and aid them to gain in all respects full acknowledgment and enjoyment of statehood, even though the persons who thus acted were but a tenth part of the original voters of their states. He would not insist upon even so many as a tenth, if only he could get *some* body of loyal citizens to deal and cooperate with in this all-important matter upon which he had set his heart; that the roster of the states might be complete again, and some healing process follow the bitter anguish of the war.

Andrew Johnson promptly made up his mind, when summoned to the presidency, to carry out Mr. Lincoln's plan, practically without modification; and he knew clearly what Mr. Lincoln's plan had been, for he himself had restored Tennessee upon that plan, as the President's agent and representative. As military governor of the state, he had successfully organized a new government out of abundant material, for Tennessee was full of men who had had no sympathy with secession; and the government which he had organized had gone into full and vigorous operation during that very spring which saw him become first Vice President, and then President. In Louisiana and Arkansas similar governments had been set up even before Mr. Lincoln's death. Congress had not recognized them,

indeed; and it did not, until a year had gone by, recognize even Tennessee, though her case was the simplest of all. Within her borders the southern revolt had been, not solid and of a piece, but a thing of frayed edges and a very doubtful texture of opinion. But, though Congress doubted, the plan had at least proved practicable, and Mr. Johnson thought it also safe and direct.

Mr. Johnson himself, unhappily, was not safe. He had been put on the same ticket with Mr. Lincoln upon grounds of expediency such as have too often created Vice Presidents of the United States. Like a great many other Tennesseeans, he had been stanch and unwavering in his adherence to the Union, even after his state had cast the Union off; but he was in all other respects a Democrat of the old order rather than a Republican of the new, and when he became President the rank and file of the Republicans in Congress looked upon him askance, as was natural. He himself saw to it, besides, that nobody should relish or trust him whom bad temper could alienate. He was self-willed, imperious, implacable; as headstrong and tempestuous as Jackson, without Jackson's power of attracting men, and making and holding parties. At first, knowing him a radical by nature, some of the radical leaders in Congress had been inclined to trust him; had even hailed his accession to the presidency with open satisfaction, having chafed under Lincoln's power to restrain them. "Johnson, we have faith in you!" Senator Wade had exclaimed. "By the gods, there will be no trouble now in running the government!" But Johnson was careful that there should be trouble. He was determined to lead as Lincoln had led, but without Lincoln's insight, skill, or sweetness of temper — by power and self-assertion rather than by persuasion and the slow arts of management and patient accommodation; and the houses came to an open breach with him almost at once.

Moreover, there was one very serious and radical objection to Mr. Lincoln's plan for restoring the states, which would in all likelihood have forced even him to modify it in many essential particulars, if not to abandon it altogether. He had foreseen difficulties, himself, and had told Congress that his plan was meant to serve only as a suggestion, around which opinion might have an opportunity to form, and out of which some practicable method might be drawn. He had not meant to insist upon it, but only to try it. The main difficulty was that it did not meet the wishes of the congressional leaders with regard to the protection of the negroes in their new rights as freemen. The men whom Mr. Lincoln had called upon to reorganize the state governments of the South were, indeed, those who were readiest to accept the results of the war, in respect of the abolition of slavery as well as in all other matters. No doubt they were in the beginning men who had never felt any strong belief in the right of secession — men who had even withstood the purpose of secession as long as they could, and had wished all along to see the old Union restored. They were a minority now, and it might be pretty safely assumed that they had been a minority from the outset in all this fatal business. But they were white men, bred to all the opinions which necessarily went along with the existence and practice of slavery. They would certainly not wish to give the negroes political rights. They might be counted on, on the contrary, to keep them still as much as possible under restraint and tutelage. They would probably accept nothing but the form of freedom for the one-time slaves, and their

rule would be doubly unpalatable to the men in the North who had gone all these weary years through, either in person or in heart, with the northern armies upon their mission of emancipation.

The actual course of events speedily afforded means for justifying these apprehensions. Throughout 1865 Mr. Johnson pushed the presidential process of reconstruction successfully and rapidly forward. Provisional governors of his own appointment in the South saw to it that conventions were elected by the voters who had taken the oath prescribed in the amnesty proclamation, which Mr. Johnson had reissued, with little change either of form or of substance; those conventions proceeded at once to revise the state constitutions under the supervision of the provisional governors, who in their turn acted now and again under direct telegraphic instructions from the President in Washington; the several ordinances of secession were repealed, the war debts of the states were repudiated, and the legislatures set up under the new constitutions hastened to accept and ratify the Thirteenth Amendment, abolishing slavery, as the President demanded. By December of the very year of his inauguration, every southern state except Florida and Texas had gone through the required process, and was once more, so far as the President was concerned, in its normal relations with the federal government. The federal courts resumed their sessions in the restored states, and the Supreme Court called up the southern cases from its docket. On December 18, 1865, the Secretary of State formally proclaimed the Thirteenth Amendment ratified by the vote of twenty-seven states, and thereby legally embodied in the Constitution, though eight of the twenty-seven were states which the President had thus of his own motion reconstructed. Without their votes the amendment would have lacked the constitutional three-fourths majority.

The President had required nothing of the new states with regard to the suffrage; that was a matter, as he truly said, in respect of which the several states had "rightfully exercised" their free and independent choice "from the origin of the government to the present day"; and of course they had no thought of admitting the negroes to the suffrage. Moreover, the new governments, once organized, fell more and more entirely into the hands of the very persons who had actively participated in secession. The President's proclamation of amnesty had, indeed, excepted certain classes of persons from the privilege of taking the oath which would make them voters again, under his arrangements for reconstruction: those who had taken a prominent official part in secession, or who had left the service of the United States for the service of the Confederate government. But a majority of the southerners were still at liberty to avail themselves of the privilege of accepting the new order of things; and it was to their interest to do so, in order that the new arrangements might be shaped as nearly as possible to their own liking. What was to their liking, however, proved as distasteful to Congress as had been expected. The use they made of their restored power brought absolute shipwreck upon the President's plans, and radically altered the whole process of reconstruction.

An extraordinary and very perilous state of affairs had been created in the South by the sudden and absolute emancipation of the negroes, and it was not strange that the southern legislatures should deem it necessary to take extraordinary steps to guard against the manifest and pressing dangers which it entailed. Here was a vast "laboring, landless, homeless class," once slaves, now free; unpracticed in liberty, unschooled in self-control; never sobered by the discipline of self-support, never established in any habit of prudence; excited by a freedom they did not understand, exalted by false hopes; bewildered and without leaders, and yet insolent and aggressive; sick of work, covetous of pleasure — a host of dusky children untimely put out of school. In some of the states they outnumbered the whites — notably in Mississippi and South Carolina. They were a danger to themselves as well as to those whom they had once served, and now feared and suspected; and the very legislatures which had accepted the Thirteenth Amendment hastened to pass laws which should put them under new restraints. Stringent regulations were adopted with regard to contracts for labor, and with regard to the prevention of vagrancy. Penalties were denounced against those who refused to work at the current rates of wages. Fines were imposed upon a great number and variety of petty offenses, such as the new freemen were most likely to commit; and it was provided that, in the (extremely probable) event of the non-payment of these fines, the culprits should be hired out to labor by judicial process. In some instances an elaborate system of compulsory apprenticeship was established for negroes under age, providing that they should be bound out to labor. In certain states the negroes were required to sign written contracts of labor, and were forbidden to do job work without first obtaining licenses from the police authorities of their places of residence. Those who failed to obtain licenses were liable to the charge of vagrancy, and upon that charge could be arrested, fined, and put to compulsory labor. There was not everywhere the same rigor; but there was everywhere the same determination to hold the negroes very watchfully, and, if need were, very sternly, within bounds in the exercise of their unaccustomed freedom; and in many cases the restraints imposed went the length of a veritable "involuntary servitude."

Congress had not waited to see these things done before attempting to help the negroes to make use of their freedom — and self-defensive use of it, at that. By an act of March 3, 1865, it established, as a branch of the War Department, a Bureau of Refugees, Freedmen, and Abandoned Lands, which was authorized and empowered to assist the one-time slaves in finding means of subsistence, and in making good their new privileges and immunities as citizens. The officials of this bureau, with the War Department behind them, had gone the whole length of their extensive authority; putting away from the outset all ideas of accommodation, and preferring the interests of their wards to the interests of peaceable, wholesome, and healing progress. No doubt that was inevitable. What they did was but the final and direct application of the rigorous, unsentimental logic of events. The negroes, at any rate, had the full advantage of the federal power. A very active and officious branch of the War Department saw to it that the new disabilities which the southern legislatures sought to put upon them should as far as possible be rendered inoperative.

That, however, did not suffice to sweeten the temper of Congress. The fact remained that Mr. Johnson had rehabilitated the governments of the southern states without asking the leave of the houses; that the legislatures which he had authorized them to call together had sought, in the very same sessions in which they gave their assent to the emancipating amendment, virtually to undo the work of emancipation, substituting a slavery of legal restraints and disabilities for a slavery of private ownership; and that these same legislatures had sent men to Washington, to seek admission to the Senate, who were known, many of them, still openly to avow their unshaken belief in the right of secession. The southern voters, too, who had qualified by taking the oath prescribed by the President's proclamation, had in most instances sent men similarly unconvinced to ask admission to the House of Representatives. Here was indeed a surrender of all the advantages of the contest of arms, as it seemed to the radicals — very generous, no doubt, but done by a Tennesseean and a Democrat, who was evidently a little more than generous; done, too, to exalt the Executive above Congress; in any light, perilous and not to be tolerated. Even those who were not radicals wished that the restoration of the states, which all admitted to be necessary, had been effected in some other way, and safeguarded against this manifest error, as all deemed it, of putting the negroes back into the hands of those who had been their masters, and would not now willingly consent to be their fellow citizens.

Congress, accordingly, determined to take matters into its own hands. With the southern representatives excluded, there was a Republican majority in both houses strong enough to do what it pleased, even to the overriding, if necessary, of the President's vetoes. Upon assembling for their regular session in December, 1865, therefore, the House and Senate at once set up, by concurrent resolution, a joint committee of nine Representatives and six Senators, which was instructed to inquire into all the conditions obtaining in the southern states, and, after sufficient inquiry, advise the houses upon the question whether, under the governments which Mr. Johnson had given them, those states were entitled to representation. To this committee, in other words, was intrusted the whole guidance of Congress in the all-important and delicate business of the full rehabilitation of the southern states as members of the Union. By February, 1866, it had virtually been settled that the admission of their representatives to Congress should await the action of the reconstruction committee; and that purpose was very consistently adhered to. An exception was made in the case of Tennessee, but in her case only. The houses presently agreed to be satisfied with her "reconstruction," and admitted her representatives to their seats in both House and Senate by an act of the 24th of July, 1865. But the other states were put off until the joint committee had forced them through a process of "Thorough," which began their reconstruction at the very beginning, again, and executed at every stage the methods preferred by the houses. The leader throughout the drastic business was Mr. Thaddeus Stevens, of Pennsylvania, the chairman of the committee, the leader of the House. He was foremost among the radicals, and drew a following about him, much as Stephen Douglas had attached thoroughgoing Democrats to himself, in the old days when the legislative battles were being fought over the extension of slavery into the territories, — by audacity, plain speaking, and the straightforward energy of unhesitating opinion. He gave directness and speed to all he proposed. He understood better than Douglas did the coarse work of hewing out practicable paths of action in the midst of opin-

ions and interests at odds. He had no timidity, no scruples about keeping to constitutional lines of policy, no regard or thought for the sensibilities of the minority — being roughhewn and without embarrassing sensibilities himself — an ideal radical for the service of the moment.

Careful men, trained in the older ways of statesmanship and accustomed to reading the Constitution into all that they did, tried to form some consistent theory of constitutional right with regard to the way in which Congress ought to deal with this new and unprecedented situation. The southern states were still "states" within the meaning of the Constitution as the Supreme Court had interpreted it. They were communities of free citizens; each had kept its territorial boundaries unchanged, unmistakable; in each there was an organized government, "sanctioned and limited by a written constitution, and established by the consent of the governed." Their officers of government, like their people, had for a time, indeed, repudiated the authority of the federal government; but they were now ready to acknowledge that authority again, and could resume their normal relations with the other states at a moment's notice, with all proper submission. Both Mr. Lincoln and Mr. Johnson had acted in part upon these assumptions. They had objected only that the governments actually in existence at the close of the war had been chosen by persons who were in fact insurgents, and that their officers had served to organize rebellion. Let those citizens of the South who had made submission, and who had been pardoned under the President's proclamation, reconstitute their governments, repudiating their old leaders, and the only taint upon their statehood would be removed: the Executive would recognize them as again normally constituted members of the Union.

Not many members of Congress, however, accepted this view. The Republican party, it was true, had entered upon the war emphatically disavowing either wish or purpose to interfere with the constitutional rights of the states; declaring its sole object to be the preservation of the Union — the denial of a single particular right which it could not but view as revolutionary. But war had brought many things in its train. The heat and struggle of those four tremendous years had burned and scarred the body of affairs with many an ineffaceable fact, which could not now be overlooked. Legally or illegally, as states or as bodies of individuals merely, the southern people had been at war with the Union; the slaves had been freed by force of arms; their freedom had now been incorporated in the supreme law of the land, and must be made good to them; there was manifest danger that too liberal a theory of restoration would bring about an impossible tangle of principles, an intolerable contradiction between fact and fact. Mr. Sumner held that, by resisting the authority of the Union, of which they were members, the southern states had simply committed suicide, destroying their own institutions along with their allegiance to the federal government. They ceased to be states, he said, when they ceased to fulfill the duties imposed upon them by the fundamental law of the land. Others declined any such doctrine. They adhered, with an instinct almost of affection, to the idea of a veritable federal Union; rejected Mr. Sumner's presupposition that the states were only subordinate parts of a consolidated national government; and insisted that, whatever rights they had for a time forfeited, the southern states were at least not destroyed, but only stopped from exercising their ordinary functions within the Union, pending a readjustment.

Theories made Mr. Stevens very impatient. It made little difference with him whether the southern states had forfeited their rights by suicide, or temporary disorganization, or individual rebellion. As a matter of fact, every department of the federal government, the courts included, had declared the citizens of those states public enemies; the Constitution itself had been for four years practically laid aside, so far as they were concerned, as a document of peace; they had been overwhelmed by force, and were now held in subjection under military rule, like conquered provinces. It was just as well, he thought, to act upon the facts, and let theories alone. It was enough that all Congressmen were agreed — at any rate, all who were allowed a voice in the matter — that it was properly the part of Congress, and not of the Executive, to bring order out of the chaos: to see that federal supremacy and federal law were made good in the South; the legal changes brought about by the war forced upon its acceptance; and the negroes secured in the enjoyment of the equality and even the privileges of citizens, in accordance with the federal guarantee that there should be a republican form of government in every state — a government founded upon the consent of a majority of its adult subjects. The essential point was that Congress, the lawmaking power, should be in control. The President had been too easy to satisfy, too prompt, and too lenient. Mr. Stevens consented once and again that the language of fine-drawn theories of constitutional right should be used in the reports of the joint Committee on Reconstruction, in which he managed to be master; but the motto of the committee in all practical matters was his motto of "Thorough," and its policy made Congress supreme.

The year 1866 passed, with all things at sixes and sevens. So far as the President was concerned, most of the southern states were already reconstructed, and had resumed their places in the Union. Their assent had made the Thirteenth Amendment a part of the Constitution. And yet Congress forbade the withdrawal of the troops, refused admittance to the southern representatives, and set aside southern laws through the action of the Freedmen's Bureau and the military authorities. By 1867 it had made up its mind what to do to bring the business to a conclusion. 1866 had at least cleared its mind and defined its purposes. Congress had still further tested and made proof of the temper of the South. In June it had adopted a Fourteenth Amendment, which secured to the blacks the status of citizens, both of the United States and of the several states of their residence, authorized a reduction in the representation in Congress of states which refused them the suffrage, excluded the more prominent servants of the Confederacy from federal office until Congress should pardon them, and invalidated all debts or obligations "incurred in aid of insurrection or rebellion against the United States"; and this amendment had been submitted to the vote of the states which Congress had refused to recognize as well as to the vote of those represented in the houses. Tennessee had promptly adopted it, and had been as promptly admitted to representation. But the other southern states, as promptly as they could, had begun, one by one, to reject it. Their action confirmed the houses in their attitude toward Reconstruction.

Congressional views and purposes were cleared the while with regard to the President, also. He had not been firm; he had been stubborn and bitter. He would yield nothing; vetoed the measures upon which Congress was most steadfastly minded to insist; alienated his very friends by attacking Congress in public with gross insult and abuse; and lost credit with everybody. It came to a direct issue, the President against Congress: they went to the country with their quarrel in the congressional elections, which fell opportunely in the autumn of 1866, and the President lost utterly. Until then some had hesitated to override his vetoes, but after that no one hesitated. 1867 saw Congress go triumphantly forward with its policy of reconstruction *ab initio*.

In July, 1866, it had overridden a veto to continue and enlarge the powers of the Freedmen's Bureau, in a bill which directed that public lands should be sold to the negroes upon easy terms, that the property of the Confederate government should be appropriated for their education, and that their newmade rights should be protected by military authority. In March, 1867, two acts, passed over the President's vetoes, instituted the new process of reconstruction, followed and completed by another act in July of the same year. The southern states, with the exception, of course, of Tennessee, were grouped in five military districts, each of which was put under the command of a general of the United States. These commanders were made practically absolute rulers, until the task of reconstruction should be ended. It was declared by the Reconstruction Acts that no other legal state governments existed in the ten states concerned. It was made the business of the district commanders to erect such governments as Congress prescribed. They were to enroll in each state, upon oath, all male citizens of one year's residence, not disqualified by reason of felony or excluded under the terms of the proposed Fourteenth Amendment, "of whatever race, color, or previous condition" they might be; the persons thus registered were to choose constitutional conventions, confining their choice of delegates to registered voters like themselves; these conventions were to be directed to frame state constitutions, which should extend the suffrage to all who had been permitted by the military authorities to enroll for the purpose of taking part in the election of delegates; and the constitutions were to be submitted to the same body of voters for ratification. When Congress had approved the constitutions thus framed and accepted, and when the legislatures constituted under them had adopted the Fourteenth Amendment, the states thus reorganized were to be readmitted to representation in Congress, and in all respects fully reinstated as members of the Union; but not before. Meanwhile, the civil governments already existing within them, though illegal, were to be permitted to stand; but as "provisional only, and in all respects subject to the paramount authority of the United States at any time to abolish, control, or supersede the same."

Such was the process which was rigorously and consistently carried through during the memorable years 1867–70; and upon the states which proved most difficult and recalcitrant Congress did not hesitate from time to time to impose new conditions of recognition and reinstatement before an end was made. By the close of July, 1868, the reconstruction and reinstatement of Arkansas, the two Carolinas, Florida, Alabama, and Louisiana had been completed. Virginia, Mississippi, and Texas were obliged to wait until the opening of 1870, because their voters would not adopt the constitutions offered them by their reconstructing conventions; and Georgia was held off a few months longer, because she persisted in attempting to exclude negroes from the right to hold office. These four states, as a consequence, were obliged to accept, as a condition precedent to their reinstatement, not only the Fourteenth Amendment, but a Fifteenth also, which Congress had passed in February, 1869, and which forbade either the United States or any state to withhold from any citizen the right to vote "on account of race, color, or previous condition of servitude." The military commanders, meanwhile, used or withheld their hand of power according to their several temperaments. They could deal with the provisional civil governments as they pleased — could remove officials, annul laws, regulate administration, at will. Some were dictatorial and petty; some were temperate and guarded in their use of authority, with a creditable instinct of statesmanship; almost all were straightforward and executive, as might have been expected of soldiers.

Whatever their mistakes or weaknesses of temper or of judgment, what followed the reconstruction they effected was in almost every instance much worse than what had had to be endured under military rule. The first practical result of reconstruction under the acts of 1867 was the disfranchisement, for several weary years, of the better whites, and the consequent giving over of the southern governments into the hands of the negroes. And yet not into their hands, after all. They were but children still; and unscrupulous men, "carpetbaggers"— men not come to be citizens, but come upon an expedition of profit, come to make the name of Republican forever hateful in the South, — came out of the North to use the negroes as tools for their own selfish ends; and succeeded, to the utmost fulfillment of their dreams. Negro majorities for a little while filled the southern legislatures; but they won no power or profit for themselves, beyond a pittance here and there for a bribe. Their leaders, strangers and adventurers, got the lucrative offices, the handling of the state moneys raised by loan, and of the taxes spent no one knew how. Here and there an able and upright man

cleansed administration, checked corruption, served them as a real friend and an honest leader; but not for long. The negroes were exalted; the states were misgoverned and looted in their name; and a few men, not of their number, not really of their interest, went away with the gains. They were left to carry the discredit and reap the consequences of ruin, when at last the whites who were real citizens got control again. . . .

J. G. Randall:

RECONSTRUCTION DÉBÂCLE

I

FOR the seceded states the Grant period constituted the darkest days of "reconstruction." Coming south after the war to make money and seize political power, the Northern "carpetbagger" became the dominant figure in Southern politics for a decade. In collusion with the carpetbaggers were the "scalawags," native whites in the South who took advantage of the chance for aggrandizement which the postwar régime offered. Southern as they were, familiar with Negro characteristics and unembarrassed by the extravagance and gaucherie of the carpetbaggers, they obtained control of numerous offices and became a power in local politics. Aided by a system which gave the vote to the Negro while it disfranchised the more substantial element among the whites, these political adventurers improved upon the system

and added extra-legal touches of their own.

Elections in the South became a byword and a travesty. Ignorant blacks by the thousands cast ballots without knowing even the names of men for whom they were voting.[1] Southern communities in their political, social, and economic interests were subjected to the misguided action of these irresponsible creatures directed by white bosses. Election laws were deliberately framed to open the way for manipulation and fraud. Ballots were inspected before going into the box, and Negroes seeking to cast Democratic ballots were held up by objections and by an effort to change their votes.[2] Registration lists showed Negroes in proportion to population at a much higher ratio

[1] W. L. Fleming, ed., *Documentary History of Reconstruction*, II, 44.

[2] *Ibid.*, II, 81–82.

From *The Civil War and Reconstruction* by J. G. Randall (Boston: D. C. Heath and Company, 1937), pp. 847–854. Used by permission.

than the actual fact. Vote-buying became so common that Negroes came to expect it; much of the bacon and ham mentioned as "relief" was distributed with an eye to election-day results.[3] To colored voters in Florida, acting under instructions from Radical leaders, the motto seemed to be "Vote early and often." Starting in early morning they moved along in groups, voting "at every precinct" on a long "line of march," each time under assumed names.[4] In advance of the voting hour ballots would be fraudulently deposited in the box. Party conventions were manipulated by Radical leaders, and nominations were forced by the bosses (sometimes military officers) in control. Reporting on the election of 1872 in Louisiana a committee of Congress stated that in their determination to have a legislature of their own party, the Republican returning board juggled election returns, accepted false affidavits, and in some cases merely estimated "what the vote ought to have been." The whole proceeding was characterized as a "comedy of blunders and frauds."[5]

By 1867 the Union League had become strongly intrenched in the South; and it proved an effective instrument in the organization of the Radical Republican party among the blacks. It was stated in October, 1867, that the League had eighty-eight chapters in South Carolina, and that almost every Negro in the state was enrolled in the order.[6] According to a statement of a Leaguer, every member was oath-bound to vote for those nominated by the order. The League, he said, existed "for no other purpose than to

carry the elections . . . ."[7] Ritual, ceremony, high-flown phrases about freedom and equal rights, sententious references to the Constitution and the Declaration of Independence, accompanied by song, prayer, and oratory, had a compelling effect upon Negro emotions, while the black man's instinctive dependence upon whites made conquest easy; so that the sanctimonious League functioned with remarkable success in capturing and delivering the Negro vote. The Leagues "voted the Negroes like 'herds of senseless cattle'" is the statement of competent observers, borne out by numerous instances similar to that of a South Carolina black who explained his vote by saying that the League was the "place where we learn the law." Another typical case was that of a Negro who was asked why he voted Republican and replied, "I can't read, and I can't write . . . . We go by instructions. We don't know nothing much."[8]

As the processes of carpetbag rule unfolded, honest men in the South felt increasing disgust. Conservative editors referred to the fancy state conventions as "black and tan" gatherings, "ring-streaked and speckled" conventions, or as assemblies of "baboons," "ragamuffins," or "jailbirds."[9] "The maddest, most . . . infamous revolution in history," was the comment of the Fairfield (South Carolina) Herald.[10] In the carpetbag constitutional convention of South Carolina (1868) 76 of the 124 delegates were colored, two-thirds of the Negroes being illiterates just emerging from slavery. These black members comported themselves in "bashful silence" while the whites attended to

[3] Ibid., II, 83.

[4] Ibid., II, 85–86.

[5] H. C. Warmoth, War, Politics and Reconstruction: Stormy Days in Louisiana, 225.

[6] Simkins and Woody, South Carolina during Reconstruction, 75 n.

[7] Ibid., 79.

[8] Ibid., 80.

[9] E. P. Oberholtzer, Hist. of the U. S. since the Civil War, II, 45.

[10] Quoted in Simkins and Woody, 110.

matters.[11] Of the whites one was put in jail for stealing his fellow members' belongings; others were accused of graver crimes; and in general it was remarked by the New York *Times* that hardly a white among the lot had a character that "would keep him out of the penitentiary."[12]

II

Supported by the Grant administration and fortified by military power, the Radical Republican state machines plunged the Southern commonwealths into an abyss of misgovernment. A congressional committee reported that one of the leading carpetbag governors made over $100,000 during his first year though his salary was $8000, while one of his appointees received fees exceeding $60,000 a year.[1] Another carpetbag governor was charged with stealing and selling the food of the freedmen's bureau intended for the relief of helpless and ragged ex-slaves. One of his associates was accused of falsely arresting Democratic members of the Florida state legislature in order to produce a carpetbag majority. F. J. Moses, scalawag, stated that he received $15,000 while governor of South Carolina for approving a large printing bill, $25,000 when speaker, and various other sums.[2]

Southern legislatures were composed largely, sometimes predominantly, of Negroes. J. S. Pike, in a passage that has become classic, described the dense Negro crowd which, amid clamor and disorder, did the debating, squabbling, and lawmaking in South Carolina. Speaker, clerk, doorkeepers, pages, and chaplain were black. No one talked more than five minutes, said Pike, without interruption. Their "bellowings and physical contortions" baffled description. It seemed to him barbarism overwhelming civilization with physical force; yet there was a curious earnestness about it all. In the confusion and uproar, with guffaws greeting the speaker as he rapped for order, the uncouth lawmakers were taking themselves seriously. "Seven years ago these men were raising corn and cotton under the whip of the overseer. To-day they are raising points of order and questions of privilege. . . . It is easier and better paid. . . . It is their day of jubilee."[3]

Some of the justices put into office by the Radicals could not write. According to a report of conditions in Mississippi, where the Ames Republicans[4] controlled the Negro vote and used it "as a solid mass," the legislature contained Negroes who could neither read nor write, members of grand juries were "totally illiterate," and the Republicans nominated as mayor of Vicksburg a man who was under indictment for twenty-three offenses.[5] Taking a leaf out of the carpetbaggers' book, Negro members of the Florida legislature were said to have formed a caucus with a "smelling committee" to "ferret out all . . . money schemes." The arrangement broke down when it was found that the colored caucus chairman appropriated to himself the moneys intended to be distributed among members for the fixing of legislative votes.[6] A

---

11 *Ibid.*, 91.

12 *Ibid.*, 92–93.

1 Fleming, *Doc. Hist.*, II, 39.

2 *Ibid.*, II, 41.

3 J. S. Pike, *The Prostrate State*, 12 ff., quoted in Fleming, *Doc. Hist.*, II, 51 ff.

4 So named after General Adelbert Ames of Maine, who was provisional governor, United States senator, and then governor of Mississippi in the carpetbag period, and under whose Radical rule there was violent opposition among the whites, leading to terrorism over the state and a serious race riot at Vicksburg on December 7, 1874.

5 Fleming, *Doc. Hist.*, II, 42–43.

6 *Ibid.*, II, 50–51.

Negro leader in South Carolina, admitting the receipt of $5000 "in connection with" legislative matters, stated that he voted for the legislative measures because he thought they were right, and that by taking the money he was keeping it in the state! Refreshments supplied at public expense to South Carolina legislators included the finest wines, ales, whiskeys, and cigars; indeed the porter thought it impossible for men to drink so much whiskey and attend to any business.[7] State house "supplies" paid for out of public funds included many varieties of liquors, costly table delicacies, luxurious furniture in lavish amounts, horses, and carriages. For the one item of printing in South Carolina the cost per month under Republican rule was more than a hundred times that of the subsequent Hampton administration. In fifteen months under the Republican administration $835,000 was spent for printing as compared to $609,000 for seventy-eight years under the old régime.[8] In the matter of "state aid" to railroad building in Alabama the notorious Stantons (John C. and Daniel N. of Boston) found their opportunity. Bringing no money into the state, they organized and promoted the Alabama and Chattanooga Railroad Company, obtained millions of state money from a bribed Radical legislature, built a hotel and opera house with some of the money, obtained fraudulent bond endorsements from the scalawag governor (William H. Smith), and left the state a wretched heritage of defaulted obligations.[9]

Huge debts were saddled upon the Southern states with the meagerest improvements to show for them. Millions in bonds in South Carolina were issued contrary to law, taxation being greatly increased, while the total assessed value of property in the state declined from $489,000,000 in 1860 to $90,000,000 in 1866.[10] Delicate women were reported selling provisions needed for their hungry children, in order to pay taxes; while for failure to pay taxes Southern whites were losing lands which were bought up by Negroes or Northern speculators.[11] South Carolina newspapers were "full of reports of sheriff's sales," 74,000 acres being put under tax sales in a brief period in Darlington County, 86,000 acres in Williamsburg County, and more than two thousand pieces of real estate in Charleston.[12] Tax rates in Mississippi were fourteen times as great in 1874 as in 1869, the public debt being piled up annually at the rate of $664,000.[13] Grants under the scalawag Holden régime to railroad companies in North Carolina exceeded $27,000,000.[14]

One of the flagrant evils of misgovernment was seen in the militia of carpetbag times. White desperadoes from Missouri, enlisted as Arkansas militiamen, tore up and down the state smashing property, destroying crops, and committing murder.[15] Groups of Negro militia in the same state became murderous mobs, with defiance born of the belief "that crimes committed . . . as a mob . . . [would] not subject them to . . . punishment."[16] A Negro militia detachment of

7 *Ibid.*, II, 59.

8 *Ibid.*, II, 69.

9 A. B. Moore, "Railroad Building in Alabama During the Reconstruction Period," *Jour. of Southern Hist.*, I, 421–441 (Nov., 1935), especially 427–430.

10 Simkins and Woody, 175.

11 *Ibid.*, 178–179.

12 *Ibid.*, 180–181.

13 Fleming, *Doc. Hist.*, II, 71.

14 J. G. de R. Hamilton, *Reconstruction in North Carolina*, 448.

15 Fleming, *Doc. Hist.*, II, 73 ff.

16 *Ibid.*, II, 77.

more than a hundred men dashed into an Arkansas town and galloped about, cursing, threatening, raiding a grocery store, and breaking into the jail.[17] Because of the terrorism practiced by the militia in North Carolina, Governor Holden was impeached and removed from office.[18] In South Carolina militia troubles developed into a war of races as outraged whites organized to protect their property and lives against armed Negro militiamen.[19] In this commonwealth the militia was almost entirely colored, and it was reported that at least two-thirds of the militia expenditures were a "huge fraud," the amount being in reality used for "political services."[20]

To use a modern phrase, government under Radical Republican rule in the South had become a kind of "racket." A parasitic organization had been grafted on to the government itself, so that the agencies of rule and authority were manipulated for private and partisan ends. Often in the reconstructed states government bore a bogus quality: that which called itself government was an artificial fabrication. Where the chance of plunder was so alluring it was no wonder that rival factions would clash for control of the spoils, nor that outraged citizens, seeking to recover the government for the people, should resort to irregular and abnormal methods. At times this clash of factions created the demoralizing spectacle of dual or rival governments. In Louisiana the Warmoth-McEnery faction battled furiously with the Kellogg-Casey faction.[21] In South Carolina "was seen

the . . . spectacle of two speakers and two Houses conducting deliberations in the same hall. Motions, . . . [etc.] were heard by the respective speakers; neither speaker, however, recognized members of the other House."[22] In Arkansas similar conditions produced the cheap melodrama of the "Brooks-Baxter war," with rival "armies" facing each other in support of their "governments," resulting in some actual bloodshed, various arrests for treason, sundry impeachments, not a little *opéra bouffe* comedy, and general confusion.[23]

Such, in brief, was the nature of carpetbag rule in the South. The concept which the Radicals sought to disseminate was that the problems of restoration had all been neatly solved, the country saved, and the South "reconstructed" by 1868. That dignified publication known as the *American Annual Cyclopedia* began its preface for the year 1868 with the following amazing statement: "This volume of the *Annual Cyclopedia*, for the year 1868, presents the complete restoration, as members of the Union, of all the Southern states except three [Virginia, Mississippi, Texas], and the final disappearance of all difficulties between the citizens of those States and the Federal Government." The fact of the matter was that this "complete restoration" was merely the beginning of the corrupt and abusive era of carpetbag rule by the forcible imposition of Radical governments upon an unwilling and protesting people. Before this imposition took place the Southern states already had satisfactory governments. It is a serious misconception to suppose that Johnson's efforts in the South had been altogether a "failure."

17 *Ibid.*, II, 76.

18 *Ibid.*, II, 78.

19 Simkins and Woody, 485.

20 Fleming, *Doc. Hist.*, II, 79.

21 See below (sec. vi of the present chapter); see also H. C. Warmoth, *War, Politics and Reconstruction . . . in Louisiana*, 233, and *passim*.

22 Simkins and Woody, 524.

23 J. M. Harrell, *The Brooks and Baxter War: A History of the Reconstruction Period in Arkansas.*

On the contrary, in the years from 1865 to 1868, when Congress had not "reconstructed" a state except Tennessee, and when state governments in the South were imperatively needed for domestic purposes, such governments were set up by Johnson. It must not be forgotten that these were native white governments genuinely supported and put into power by the Southern people, and that they functioned in the preservation of order and internal government in those important years that intervened between the surrenders and the establishment of carpetbag misrule by Congress. If one would seek to measure the importance of this, let him contemplate what would have been the result if these commonwealths had made no such adjustment and had waited several years for Congress to supply the pattern for state governments. Instead of saying that reconstruction had been solved by Congress in 1868, the truer generalization would be that the transition to normal polity in the South had been pretty well worked out by Johnson, that it was violently interrupted by the Radicals, and that only

after the overthrow of the Radical régime (about 1877) did genuine political reconstruction get under way with any fair prospect for the future.

Another unfair conclusion is to attribute the excesses of the carpetbag period to the Negro. Though the Radicals used Negro voting and officeholding for their own ends, Republican governments in the South were not Negro governments. Even where Negroes served, the governments were under white control. It is the contention of Carter G. Woodson that "most of the local offices . . . were held by the white men, and [that] those Negroes who did attain some of the higher offices were . . . about as competent as the average whites thereto elected." He also argues that illiteracy among Negro officeholders has been exaggerated.[24] That the first phase of the Negro's experience of freedom after centuries of slavery should occur under the degrading conditions of these carpetbag years was not the fault of the Negro himself, but of the whites who exploited him. . . .

[24] Carter G. Woodson, *The Negro in Our History*, 403 ff.

Roger W. Shugg:
CLASS AND RACE STRIFE IN LOUISIANA

. . . **MILITARY** reconstruction reduced all the former states of the Confederacy except Tennessee to the status of conquered territory, which could regain their sovereignty only by obedience to the dictates of Congress,

enlargement of the suffrage to include Negroes, and ratification of the Fourteenth Amendment.[1] To fulfill these con-

[1] The three reconstruction acts of 1867 which made this policy law are to be found in *U. S. Statutes at Large*, XIV, 428 ff., XV, 2 ff., 14 ff.

Roger W. Shugg, *Origins of Class Struggle in Louisiana* (Baton Rouge: Louisiana State University Press, 1939), pp. 219–232. Used by permission.

ditions in Louisiana, a constituent assembly was elected by all "loyal" men on a war basis, for loyalty was interpreted by General Sheridan as barring Confederate veterans and Democratic officeholders from the polls.[2] A contemporary newspaper estimated that half the white citizens were disfranchised.[3] Whatever the number who were disqualified, and it must have been large, the registration was heavily colored.[4] No one was surprised that radicals elected to the Convention of 1868 all but two of their candidates.[5]

The local Republicans who thus won control of Louisiana had organized their party in 1865. Thomas Durant, an old Douglas Democrat, presided at its first convention. Henry Clay Warmoth, a poor, white lawyer of Southern ancestry who was more a scalawag than a carpetbagger, became its moving spirit. His program from the start was one of radical reconstruction; he promoted it unofficially on the floor of Congress,[6] and came into power when this body made it law. The original party membership was composed of free men of color, emigrants from the North, demobilized Federal soldiers, and native unionists. Northerners were always influential but never in the majority; as late as 1874 there were only about seven thousand voters who confessed to having been born Yankees.[7] The strength of the party at the polls

rested with the colored masses.[8] To carry the Convention of 1868, over fifty thousand freedmen were organized in a Republican Loyal League.[9]

With the elevation of this race from slavery to free suffrage, the revolution entered its second stage: black labor was ostensibly in a position to control the state. It might be supposed that the Negro would rule the Republican party, not only by the sheer weight of his numerical preponderance, but also because he was led by educated mulattoes such as Oscar Dunn and P. B. S. Pinchback, a type which was the peculiar product of ante-bellum racial relations in Louisiana. That this was not to be the case became apparent early in the Convention of 1868. The delegates elected to this assembly had been drawn equally from both races by agreement of the party chiefs in order to avoid conflicts of color.[10] The important committee to draft a constitution was nevertheless composed of five white and four colored members, who divided by race and submitted different reports. The document which finally emerged from the convention was the product of many compromises, but followed essentially the recommendations of the white majority.[11] The Negroes suffered another loss when their gubernatorial candidate was defeated by Warmoth on a ballot polled according to color; their nominee was then satisfied with the Lieutenant-Governorship.[12] The colored delegates sustained additional defeats when they lost

2 Fleming, *Documentary History of Reconstruction*, I, 433–35.

3 *Times*, Apr. 21, 1867.

4 Cf. Lonn, *Reconstruction in Louisiana after 1868*, 5.

5 Ficklen, *History of Reconstruction . . .* , 193. With the colored registration alone amounting to 82,907, there were 75,083 votes cast in favor of holding the convention.

6 H. C. Warmoth, *War, Politics and Reconstruction; etc.* (New York, 1930), 43–45.

7 *Rpt. State Registrar of Voters, 1874*, Table 2.

8 Nordhoff, *The Cotton States in the Spring and Summer of 1875*, 41.

9 *Republican*, Nov. 17, 1867.

10 Ficklen, *History of Reconstruction*.

11 Du Bois, *Black Reconstruction*, 468.

12 Warmoth, *op. cit.*, 54–55. The vote was close, 45–43. A mulatto, Oscar Dunn, honest and intelligent, was nominated for Lieutenant-Governor.

their fight for agrarian legislation,[13] and against drastic disfranchisement of their former masters.[14] Henceforth the Negroes who had been "Pure Radicals" failed to take the lead in shaping the policy of their party. In vain they had boasted "we have more than the ballot: we compose a majority in the State, and with the help of our Radical white friends . . . the colored masses are the masters of the field."[15] White Republicans led by Warmoth, Casey, Carter, Kellogg, and Packard became the masters of reconstruction and ruled the state with the support of colored officeholders and voters, and the protection of Federal troops.

The Constitution of 1868 nevertheless gave the Negro many nominal advantages, several of which actually worked to his disadvantage. Although he had but recently emerged from a servile condition of enforced ignorance, and was on the whole illiterate, he was granted the right to vote and to hold any office in the state.[16] These dubious privileges only made him the tool of others until he became intelligent enough to have a will and understanding of his own.[17] For the convention it was enough to open all public schools to freedmen,[18] though five

delegates warned their colleagues that to mix the races in this way and to waive all color discrimination would be to wreck the educational system.[19]

No less disastrous for the immediate future of the Negro was the convention's unqualified declaration of social equality,[20] which aroused greater resentment among white people than colored suffrage. It was adopted largely by colored votes at the insistence of Pinchback.[21] The abolition of civil and social discrimination was difficult to challenge in theory and as a principle of abstract right.[22] But the traditions and temper of popular white opinion made all questions relating to the freedman a race problem, not one of philosophical doctrine or politics. It was widely believed, even by sensible people, that if the Negro could ride with them in street cars and sit next to their children at school, there would be nothing to prevent miscegenation.[23] The colored press replied that these apprehensions were unjustified, and that Democrats deliberately inflamed them in order to regain political control. Social equality meant nothing more to the intelligent Negro than the right of any man, whatever his color, to come and go in public places, and to pursue his own happiness, provided he did not infringe the equal right of another. There was no thought of racial intermarriage, even among the uneducated, but only of the admission of freedmen to civil society so that they might be free to walk the streets, fre-

[13] See below, Chap. VIII.

[14] Russ, "Disfranchisement in Louisiana (1862–70)," *L.H.Q.*, XVIII (July, 1935), 575–576. Pinchback declared himself opposed to this measure, Article 99, because he believed "that two-thirds of the colored men of this State do not desire disfranchisement to such a great extent."

[15] *Tribune*, Oct. 30, 1867.

[16] *Const. 1868*, Arts. 2, 98.

[17] Cf. R. Taylor's illuminating report of his conversation with Charles Sumner on this subject for a revelation of the *non sequitur* in radical thought, *Destruction and Reconstruction*, 245.

[18] Unfortunately for both races the convention rejected a proposal, 56–8, to restrict suffrage after 1872 to the literate. *Official Journal of the Proceedings of the Convention for Framing a*

Constitution for the State of Louisiana (New Orleans, 1867–68), 175.

[19] *Ibid.*, 200–1.

[20] *Const. 1868*, Art. 13.

[21] *Const. Conv. J.*, 1868, 242–43. It was passed, 58–16, and opened public places to both races. Ficklen, *History of Reconstruction*, 198.

[22] *Ibid.*, 291–92.

[23] *Tribune*, Apr. 14; *Times*, May 6, 1867.

quent public institutions, attend schools, and appear in courts of law like other citizens.[24] But white members of the convention who were sympathetic to the aspirations of colored people protested that there was no use in making laws so far in advance of public opinion.[25] Such doctrines were especially offensive to white farmers and laborers, who saw no good in the Constitution of 1868.

This document was hailed by colored radicals as "the deathblow of the slave oligarchy in Louisiana."[26] Their optimism was justified in so far as the old leaders of the state, the planters and merchants, were temporarily disfranchised and their ballots handed over to those who had formerly been their slaves. The power to make laws was ostensibly reposed with a colored majority, for seats in both houses were allotted according to total population.[27] This revival of the 1852 basis of representation was bitterly resented by white people, because the colored were no longer merely counted but actually allowed to vote and represent themselves. Although the black belt possessed no more legislative seats than before the war,[28] the majority of Negroes in this region, and not a minority of white planters, were now in a position to control legislation. This obliteration of the color line which had previously determined who should constitute a majority in the state led to a fierce struggle between blacks and whites. Peace was to be restored only with the triumph of white supremacy in 1877.

For nine years previous to this date, however, Louisiana was in the grip of carpetbag government. Its political structure, based on the Constitution of 1868, was strong because it centralized "imperial power in the governor's hands."[29] The degree to which he controlled the state became extraordinary as one law after another augmented his overlordship. It is notable that the only opposition to him within the government arose from the Custom House, because he did not administer Federal patronage.[30] In the state he was supreme. He was able to appoint and remove local registrars of voters, tax collectors, and assessors, besides the board of public works and metropolitan police officers for New Orleans; he could name special constables with power to make summary arrests everywhere, and fill all vacancies of office, even in parish police juries.[31] If a hostile judge should be elected to any court, the legislature would gerrymander his district, as in New Orleans, and create a new one, to which the governor forthwith appointed a friendly judge.[32] Elections "were a farce," since "the governor appointed the registrars, and through them returned his friends to the legislature."[33] The registration never tallied with tax or census figures, and in some places embraced more Negroes than were alive. It was easy for corrupt voters to repeat and stuff the ballot box since a citizen could use any poll in his parish or — in New Orleans — in his ward.[34] Whatever the actual vote, a central returning board, composed of a Republican majority confirmed by the Senate, could

24 *Le Progrès de St. Landry*, Sept. 12, 1868.
25 *Const. Conv. J.*, 1868, 275–77.
26 *St. Landry Progress*, Apr. 11, 1868.
27 *Const. 1868*, Arts. 21, 30.
28 Cf. *U. S. Cen.*, 1860, *Prelim. Rpt.*, 262; *Const. 1868*, Art. 22.

29 *Affairs in Louisiana*, 42 Cong., 2 sess. [1872], H. Rpts., no. 92, p. 21, minority rpt.
30 See Lonn, *Reconstruction in Louisiana after 1868* (New York, 1918), IV, 73 ff.
31 Nordhoff, *op. cit.*, 44.
32 *Ibid.*, 46–47.
33 See above, n. 29.
34 Nordhoff, *op. cit.*, 65.

change the results to suit its own rules of political arithmetic.[35]

This gubernatorial despotism was the antithesis of democratic government. It gave one man, at first H. C. Warmoth and then W. P. Kellogg, the control of elections, courts, and taxation; and by his leadership of the Republican party, he dominated the legislature and the making of laws. The governor was generally supported in the face of local opposition by President Grant, who maintained a "Federal protectorate" over Louisiana with national troops.[36] The state was policed for a decade by soldiers whose mission was to preserve law and order, especially at elections, but the law was whatever a corrupt legislature ratified, elections were determined by fraudulent returns, and the overseer of Louisiana was the governor.

There were nevertheless said to be permanent benefits which accrued from misrule of this type, especially in South Carolina and Mississippi, but they were overlooked until one historian called attention to them in 1910.[37] He claimed that during this period the South achieved democratic government, free public schools, and important social legislation.[38] If these reforms were introduced into other states,[39] Louisiana was conspicuous for their absence. Government became nominally democratic by the Constitution of 1868, as we have seen, but in practice it proved to be despotic. The free public schools which had been established in 1844, and were now open

to both races, suffered almost complete collapse because of racial prejudice, fraud, and inefficiency.[40] Of effective social legislation, there was none. When Nordhoff examined the statutes enacted during reconstruction, he "met with dozens of petty swindles," and reached the conclusion that "a more amusing and preposterous exhibition of wholesale legislative plundering it would be difficult to imagine."[41]

Anyone who goes through the sessional laws of this period will confirm Nordhoff's opinion. The overwhelming bulk of the legislation divided itself into two categories, political and economic, which had the single aim of maintaining in power Republican politicians and rewarding their friends. Whether it was the creation of a new parish like Grant, for exploitation by carpetbaggers as notorious as the Twitchells, or the issue of railway, land, and improvement bonds, the telltale mark of fraud was upon each law. There would be no point in a tedious explanation of these corrupt statutes,[42] especially when the truth of their unsavory negotiation, shrouded in discreet mystery from the start, has been forever lost.

It is more important to realize that no race, class, or party could lay a virtuous claim to clean hands. In each case the majority were honest, of course, if only because they were powerless or indifferent. But politicians bribed legislators for party and parish favors, and business men and corporations bribed the politicians for economic privileges.[43] There

[35] *Ibid.*

[36] *Ibid.*, 68.

[37] W. E. B. Du Bois, "Reconstruction and Its Benefits," *A.H.R.*, XV (July, 1910), 781–99.

[38] *Ibid.*, 795–96.

[39] Cf. F. B. Simkins and R. H. Woody, *South Carolina during Reconstruction*, which is a pioneer work on this and other questions.

[40] *Rpt. State Supt. Pub. Educ., 1872, passim;* 1877, *passim.*

[41] *Op. cit.*, 60–62.

[42] Cf. Nordhoff, *loc. cit.*

[43] "The legislative corruption involves both parties. Among the principal movers in legislative jobs were wealthy, influential, and highly re-

was some truth in Governor Warmoth's speech to the bankers who were lobbying to protect and advance their interests. "I tell you," he said, "these much-abused members of the Louisiana legislature are at all events as good as the people they represent. Why, damn it, everybody is demoralizing down here. Corruption is the fashion."[44] In these circumstances even the honorable business man had to resort to bribery to avoid political reprisals and to pay off legislative blackmail, and prices were high because corruption was rampant. But it should be remembered, as Du Bois observed, that colored men obtained only a small share of the graft, which was designated in legislative accounts as "sundries and incidentals," while white men took the lion's share of state bonds, warrants, charters, and land.[45]

Carpetbag rule was eventually caught in two dilemmas, and its failure to solve them provoked violent opposition which led ultimately to its downfall. First was the fact that its electoral majorities consisted of colored votes: without support of the Negro at the polls, radicals could not obtain office; but to rely on the ballots of one race, and that the weaker, was to unite the other and stronger race in implacable hostility; and the Negro would prove to be unreliable in the face of such enemies, because whatever his political allegiance, his economic necessities bound him to the white planter.

Second was the no less important fact that carpetbag government fed on cor-ruption; since radicals lacked the confidence of business or white citizens, and depended on the protection of the Federal army for their precarious tenure of power, they could not draw their party funds and individual perquisites from the economic development of the state. So they turned to political exploitation and feathered their nests directly from the public revenue, which raised taxes higher without increasing receipts, further depressed trade and agriculture, and completed the process of alienating the white electorate. Each dilemma was inescapable; the first was of a racial and social character, the second, racial and economic; together they issued in the race strife, apparently more social than economic, which finally put an end to carpetbag rule.

Oppressive taxation was largely responsible for bringing men of property and influence into violent collision with the radicals. The rate for the state jumped from 37½ cents on $100 in 1866 to $2.15 in 1871.[46] Notwithstanding these increased levies, the debt rose from about eleven millions after the war to over fifty millions in 1875. There was also a rapid rise in the local rates for most parishes. In Natchitoches, for example, where $13,475 had been sufficient revenue in 1860, the sum of $82,207 was not enough in 1873 to cover local expenses and peculations.[47] These heavy fiscal demands were made of a people who had not recovered from the losses of war before they were further depressed by the Panic of 1873. The consequences for New Orleans were disastrous. Here the value of residential property was cut in half, and the sheriff made more than 47,000 seizures for taxes from 1871 through

spectable democrats." *Affairs in Louisiana*, 42 Cong., 2 sess. [1872], *H. Rpts.*, IV, no. 92, p. 37; separate dissent by H. B. Smith. See Warmoth's testimony on Democratic votes for four railway subsidies, *ibid.*, 38–39.

[44] *Rpt. . . . on . . . Condition of the South*, 43 Cong., 2 sess. [1875], *H. Rpts.*, V, no. 261, pt. iii, 973.

[45] *Op. cit.*, 792.

[46] *Rpt. . . . on . . . Condition of the South*, 974.

[47] Nordhoff, *op. cit.*, 54.

1873.[48] The situation was no better in the country.[49] It was especially hard for "small farmers," according to Nordhoff, because they were "forced to pay the heavy taxes, while in many cases their rich neighbors resist."[50] The fiscal crisis had become acute by 1872.

It was truly said that "office-holders grow rich, while the people are impoverished." With "capital . . . flying from the State, [and] commerce . . . decreasing,"[51] resistance to confiscatory taxation spread far and wide. A league was formed in New Orleans and the rural parishes to refuse all payments, and merchants and planters were foremost in this rebellion.[52] Some fifty-five lawyers in New Orleans offered to defend tax suits without charge.[53] The movement coincided with the first vigorous and united election campaign by the whites against carpet-bag rule in 1872. It can hardly be doubted that the resistance to taxation inspired a relentless struggle for home rule.[54] The "same old crew of political buzzards and insatiable jackals who have robbed and plundered us to the verge of bankruptcy, and paralyzed all industry in the State,"[55] could not be borne for long if agriculture and trade were to survive.

While it was chiefly the propertied citizens who rebelled against the oppressive taxation of reconstruction, the poor and white were stirred no less by pride of race and hatred of any Negro who attempted to rule them. Where parish officials happened to be colored, as in Natchitoches or St. Landry, murders and riots were frequent.[56] It was an unpleasant sight for a poor white farmer to watch a poor Negro grow prosperous in public office, and galling to him to pay the taxes which were too often the source of his prosperity.[57] The colored men who were corrupt, ignorant, dissolute, and bold, though a very small minority, earned for their race the distrust and contempt of the white man.

In the rural parishes the hard-working farmers sometimes lost their patience and carried out with violence or intimidation the desperate threats uttered by propertied men or abusive newspapers.[58] It was the poor white men, to judge by the comparative poverty of such a large proportion of the people after the war,[59] who made up the forces which struggled under McEnery, Ogden, and Nicholls to restore Democratic home rule. They figured in the savage race riots at Colfax in 1873, and Coushatta in 1874,[60] marched among the five thousand citizens who participated in the New Orleans uprising of September 14, 1874,[61] and filled the ranks of the White League.

---

48 *Ibid.*, 62–63.

49 See below, chap. VIII.

50 *Op. cit.*, 59.

51 *Affairs in Louisiana*, 21, 29, testimony of J. B. Eustis.

52 *Rpt. . . . on . . . Condition of the South*, 965.

53 *Ibid.*, 963.

54 *Natchitoches Vindicator*, quoted in *ibid.*, 921–27.

55 *Alexandria Caucasian*, quoted in *ibid.*, 767.

56 This state of affairs continued, even without colored officials to incite them, to 1878. See the partisan but revealing *Rpt. . . . into Alleged Frauds and Violence in the Elections of 1878, etc.*, 45 Cong., 3 sess. [1879], *Sen. Rpts.*, IV, no. 855, pt. i; for Caddo, 3–110, 589–93; Natchitoches, 115–66, 484–558; Tensas, 169–354, 453–83; Concordia, 355–78; St. Mary, 381–96; Pt. Coupee, 411–29.

57 Interview with H. L. Brian, May 2, 1933.

58 The *Shreveport Times*, under the vehement editorship of Leonard, set the tone for the country press in the northern parishes.

59 See below, chaps. VIII, IX.

60 See H. O. Lestage, Jr., "The White League in Louisiana and Its Participation in Reconstruction Riots," *L.H.Q.*, XVIII (July, 1935), 619–93.

61 *Commercial Bulletin*, Sept. 13, 14; *Picayune*, Sept. 14; *Times*, Sept. 14, 1874; quoted in *Rpt.*

It is impossible to estimate the strength or to exaggerate the importance of an organization like the White League. When the New Orleans *Bulletin* put its enrollment at fourteen thousand men, "organized and armed," a North Louisiana paper claimed that there were at least ten thousand men who belonged to it in that region alone.[62] The support of newspapers in every part of the state indicated how widespread and strong the movement was.[63] Its temper was desperate, and grew especially bitter in 1874. Two years before, President Grant had robbed the McEnery-Warmoth coalition of their apparent electoral victory and placed Governor Kellogg in power with national troops.[64] The Louisiana Democrats, encouraged by national party successes in the lower house of Congress, were resolved to throw off the yoke of carpetbag rule. *"We intend to succeed by intimidation,"* not with guns but with a virtuous cause, declared the New Orleans *Times.*[65] But the Shreveport *Times* gave voice to the force which lay behind this peaceable profession: "If a single gun is fired between the whites and blacks in this and surrounding parishes, *every carpetbagger and scalawag that can be caught will in twelve hours therefrom be dangling from a limb."*[66]

The local political parties, Democratic or "people's" and Republican, had divided the races and set them against one another.[67] Economic coercion of the Negro on the plantations, to change his allegiance or persuade him to be neutral, was approved and widely practiced.[68] Thus the stage was set for the overthrow of carpetbag government and the restoration of white supremacy.[69] All that was needed was a change in the national government, the succession of Hayes to the Presidency, to withdraw Federal soldiers in 1877, for they were the last mainstay of carpetbag rule.

"To use a modern phrase," remarks a recent historian, "government under Radical Republican rule in the South had become a kind of 'racket.' "[70] Charles Nordhoff, an intelligent observer who was the less prejudiced because he had been brought up to hate slavery and sympathize with the Negro, entered an eloquent judgment on conditions in Louisiana which has not been altered by research. A "small band of white men," he wrote in 1875, "have for more than six years monopolized all political power and preferment in the State. They have laid, collected and spent (and largely misspent) all the taxes, local taxes as well as State; they have not only made all the laws, but they have arbitrarily changed them, and have miserably failed to enforce any which were for the people's good; they have openly and scandalously corrupted the colored men whom they have brought into political life; they have used unjust laws to perpetuate and extend their own power; and they have practiced all the basest arts

---

... on ... *Condition of the South,* 798–807, 814–34.

[62] *Minden Democrat,* Aug. 29, 1874, quoted in *ibid.,* 792.

[63] See citations from nine newspapers in *ibid.,* 764–68, 770–72.

[64] Randall, *The Civil War and Reconstruction* (Boston, 1937), 869.

[65] Aug. 5, 1874, quoted in *Rpt. . . . on . . . Condition of the South* [1875], 765.

[66] July 29, 1874, quoted in *ibid.*

[67] See the Baton Rouge platform of the white coalition "opposed to the Kellogg usurpation," in *Picayune,* Aug. 26, 1874, quoted in *ibid.,* 908–9. The Republican chairman, Packard, told Nordhoff, *op. cit.,* 41, that only about five thousand whites voted this party's ticket by 1874.

[68] E.g., *Shreveport Times,* Oct. 14, 1874.

[69] Randall, *loc. cit.*

[70] Randall, *op. cit.,* 852.

of ballot-stuffing, false registration, and repeating, at election after election."[71] It was gang rule, the kind of government to which American cities were accus-

71 *Op. cit.*, 43.

tomed, but which had never seized a state with such flagrant impunity and ease until the destruction of reconstruction was visited upon Louisiana by misguided national politics and politicians.

Walter L. Fleming:

CIVIL WAR AND RECONSTRUCTION IN ALABAMA

Taxation During Reconstruction

AFTER the war it was certain that taxation would be higher and expenditure greater, both on account of the ruin caused by the war that now had to be repaired, and because several hundred thousand negroes had been added to the civic population. Before the war the negro was no expense to the state and county treasuries; his misdemeanors were punished by his master. Yet neither the ruined court-houses, jails, bridges, roads, etc., nor the criminal negroes can account for the taxation and expenditure under the carpet-bag régime. During the three and a half years after the war, under the provisional governments, most of the burned bridges, court-houses, and other public buildings had been replaced; and there were relatively few negroes who were an expense to the carpet-bag government.

After the overthrow of Reconstruction, Governor Houston stated that the total value of all property in Alabama in 1860 was $725,000,000, and that in 1875 it was

$160,000,000.[1] In 1866 the assessed valuation was $123,946,475;[2] in 1870 it was $156,770,385,[3] and in 1876, after ten years of Reconstruction, it was $135,535,792.[4] Before the war the taxes were paid on real estate and slaves. In 1860 the taxes were paid upon slave property assessed at $152,278,000, and upon real estate assessed at $155,034,000.[5]

Although there was some property left in 1865, the owners could barely pay taxes on it. The bank capital was gone, and no one had money that was receivable for taxes. Consequently, it was impossible to collect general taxes, and the state government was obliged to place

1 Senate Journal, 1875–1876, p. 214.

2 Ku Klux Rept., p. 171.

3 Ku Klux Rept., p. 318.

4 Auditor's Report, 1902, p. 19.

5 Ku Klux Rept., p. 170; Census of 1860. The assessed valuation of property increased 117% from 1850 to 1860. The comptroller's report of Nov. 12, 1858, states that the slave property of the state at that time paid nearly half the taxes. This was true of all ordinary taxes to 1865. See Senate Journal, 1866–1867, p. 291.

Walter L. Fleming, *Civil War and Reconstruction in Alabama* (New York: Peter Smith, 1949), pp. 571–582. Used by permission.

temporary loans and levy license taxes. No regular taxes were collected during 1865 and 1866. The first regular tax was levied in 1866, and was collected in time to be spent by the Reconstruction convention.[6] For four years after the surrender the crops were bad, and when called good they were hardly more than half of the crops of 1860.[7] However, if no state taxes were paid by the impoverished farmers, there still remained the heavy Federal tax of $12.50 to $15 per bale on all cotton produced.

The rate of taxation before the war on real estate and on slaves was one-fifth of one per cent. After the war the taxes were raised by the provisional government to one-fourth of one per cent, and license taxes were added. The reconstructed government at once raised the rate to three-fourths of one per cent on property of all descriptions,[8] and added

new license taxes, more than quadrupling the former rate. Under Lindsay, the Democratic governor in 1871–1872, the rate was lowered to one-half of one per cent. The assessment of property under Reconstruction was much more stringent than before. There were only five other states that paid a tax rate as high as three-fourths of one per cent, and four of these were southern states.[9]

Before the war the county tax was usually 60 per cent of the state tax, never more. The city and town tax was insignificant. After the war the town and city taxes were greatly increased, the county tax was invariably as much as the state tax, and many laws were passed authorizing the counties to levy additional taxes and to issue bonds. The heaviest burdens were from local taxation, not from state taxes.[10] In Montgomery County, the county taxes before the war had never been more than $30,000, and had been paid by slaveholders and owners of real estate. During Reconstruction the taxes were never less than $90,000, and every one except the negroes had to pay on everything that was property. In fact, the taxes in this county were about quadrupled.[11] In Marengo County the taxes before the war were $12,000; after 1868

---

[6] Journal Convention of 1867, p. 125; Patton's Report to the Convention, Nov. 11, 1867.

[7] Cotton crop, 1860 .... 842,729 bales
Cotton crop, 1865 .... 75,305 bales
Cotton crop, 1866 .... 429,102 bales
Cotton crop, 1867 .... 239,516 bales
Cotton crop, 1868 .... 366,193 bales
Most of the war crop was confiscated by the United States. The crops of 1866–1868 show the effects of politics among the negro laborers rather than unfavorable seasons. Hodgson, "Alabama Manual and Statistical Register," 1869.

[8] The exemption laws were so framed as to release the average negroes from paying tax, and also the class of whites that supported the Radical policy. The following list will show the incidence of taxation for 1870: —

	Value	Tax
Lands	$81,109,102.03	$607,979.52
Town property	36,005,780.50	268,865.89
Cattle	1,180,106.00	8,851.36
Mules	4,845,736.00	36,042.68
Horses	2,214,376.00	16,599.83
Sheep and goats	111,001.00	832.50
Hogs	277,735.50	2,083.02
Wagons, carriages, etc.	131,235.00	8,480.81
Tools	237,534.50	1,769.96
Farming Implements	235,600.00	1,744.71
Household furniture	1,691,807.00	12,731.98
Cotton presses	41,360.00	310.30

Besides these items, heavy taxes were laid on the following: wharves, toll bridges, ferries,

steamboats, and all water craft, stocks of goods, libraries, jewellery, plate and silverware, musical instruments, pistols, guns, jacks and jennies, racehorses, watches, money in and out of the state, money loaned, credits, commercial paper, capital in incorporated companies in or out of the state, bonds except of United States and Alabama, income and gains over $1000, banks, poll tax, insurance companies, auction sales, lotteries, warehouses, distilleries, brokers, factors, express and telegraph companies, etc. See Ku Klux Report and Auditor's Report, 1871.

[9] Revenue Laws of Ala., 1865–1870; Report of the Debt Commission, Jan. 24, 1876; Governor Lindsay's Message, Nov. 21, 1871; Ku Klux Rept., Ala. Test., pp. 227, 340, 976, 1056, 1504.

[10] See Acts of Ala., 1868–1874, *passim.*

[11] Ku Klux Rept., Ala. Test., pp. 240, 360.

they were $25,000 to $30,000, notwithstanding the fact that property had depreciated two-thirds in value since the
war. Land worth formerly $50 to $60 an
acre now sold for $3 to $15.[12] In Madison County, the state taxes in 1858 were
$23,417.63 (gross); in 1870, $66,745.53
(net). The state land tax in 1858 in the
same county was $7,213.10; in 1870, $51,-
445.30. Madison County taxes were: —

	In 1859	In 1869
State Tax	$26,633.71	$65,410.85
County Tax	13,316.85	65,410.85
Total	$39,950.56	$130,821.70

The general testimony was that the
exemption laws relieved from taxation
nearly all the negroes, except those who
paid taxes before the war.[13]

The following table will show the taxation for 1860 and 1870: —

	1860	1870
Census Valuation	$432,198,762[14]	$156,770,387
State Tax	530,107	1,477,414
County Tax	309,474	1,122,471
Town Tax	11,590	430,937

Administrative Expenses

Table of Receipts and Expenditures of the
State Government

Year	Receipts	Expenditures
1860	......	$530,107.00
1865	$1,626,782.93[15]	2,282,355.97[15]
1866	62,967.80[16]	606,494.39[17]
1867	691,048.86	819,434.85[18]
1868	724,760.56[19]	1,066,860.24[19]
1868	1,788,982.43[19]	2,233,781.97[19]
1869	686,451.02[20]	1,394,960.30
1870	1,283,586.52	1,336,398.85
1871	1,422,494.67[21]	1,640,116.99[22]
1872	......	......
1873	2,081,649.39	2,237,822.06[23]
1874	......	......
1875	725,000.00	500,000.00[24]
1876	781,800.64	682,591.49
1886	888,724.33	818,366.70

12 Ala. Test., pp. 1303, 1304.

13 Ala. Test., pp. 461, 963, 964.

14 Taxes were paid on $307,312,000, slaves in-
cluded; see Census of 1860; Census of 1870; Ku
Klux Rept., pp. 170, 171, 175, 317, 318.

15 Includes receipts and disbursements in Confederate money.

The average yearly cost of state,
county, and town administration from
1858 to 1860 was $800,000; from 1868 to
1870, the average cost of the state administration alone was $1,107,080, the
cost of state, county, and town government being at least $3,000,000.[25] The pro-
visional state government disbursed in
the year 1866–1867, $676,476.54, of which
only $262,627.47 was spent for state
expenses; the remainder was used for
schools.[26]

The greater expenditure of the Reconstruction government can, in small part,
be explained by the greater number of
officials and by the higher salaries paid.[27]

16 License taxes only.

17 License taxes, bond issues, and temporary
loans.

18 Interest paid on the public debt with bond
issues included, and expenses of the convention
of 1867. The actual expenses of the state administration were $262,627.47.

19 The first figures for 1868 include the receipts
from taxes and the expenditures for state purposes only; the other figures include the proceeds
from sale of bonds used for state purposes. The
Radicals always gave the first set of figures, and
the Democrats the second.

20 $620,000 should be added for the sale of bonds
and state obligations.

21 Issue of bonds to railroads included.

22 Includes interest paid on railroad bonds.

23 Currency had depreciated. Many claims
went unpaid. The "home debt" amounted to
$823,454.64. The actual state expenses were
$1,384,044.46.

24 State expenses only. Democrats in power. See
Auditor's Reports, 1869–1873, 1900; Ku Klux
Rept., pp. 170, 174, 176, 1055, 1057; Report of
the Debt Commission, 1876; Journal Convention
of 1867, p. 125.

25 Ku Klux Rept., pp. 170, 174, 176; Auditor's
Reports, 1869–1870; Reports of the Alabama
Debt Commission.

26 Report of Governor Patton to the Convention,
Nov. 11, 1867; Journal Convention of 1867, p.
125.

27 See Tuskegee News, June 3, 1875; Auditor's
Reports, 1868–1874.

Salaries

	Before the War	During Reconstruction
Governor	$2,000.00	$4,000.00
Governor's clerk ...	500.00	5,400.00‡
Secretary of State .	1,200.00	2,400.00§
Treasurer	1,800.00	2,800.00
Departmental clerks	1,000.00*	1,500.00
Supreme Court judge	3,000.00	4,000.00
Circuit judges	13,500.00	36,000.00
Chancellors	4,500.00†	15,000.00
Member of Legislature, *per diem* ..	4.00	6.00
Stationary executive departments	1,200.00	12,708.77[28]

* each   † three   ‡ two   § fees and charges

The administration of Lindsay to a great extent had to pay the debts of the former administration. Expenses were curtailed when possible, and notwithstanding the fact that the indorsed railroads defaulted in 1871, the business of the state was conducted much more economically, and there were fewer and smaller issues of bonds and obligations.[29] The Senate, however, had but one Democrat in it, and the House was only doubtfully Democratic, as the Democratic members were young and inexperienced men or else discontented scalawags.[30] Consequently, the tide of corruption and extravagance was merely checked, not stopped. The capitol expenses of Smith and of Lindsay for a year make an instructive comparison: —

	Governor Smith 1869–1870	Governor Lindsay 1871–1872
Contingent expenses .	$47,197.28	$20,531.84
Stationery, fuel, etc. .	24,310.07	8,847.23
Clerical services	27,883.77	21,883.03
Public printing	80,279.18	49,716.43

[28] The average legislator in 1872–1873 was paid $904.00 and mileage. The Senate had 33 members and 44 attending officers, clerks, and secretaries; the lower house, with a membership of 100, had from 77 to 84 attending officials. Besides these there were dozens of pages, doorkeepers, firemen, assistants, etc. In 1869 there were 105 regular capitol servants who received $31,900 in wages. Auditor's Report, 1869–1873;

Other expenses, in so far as they were under the control of Lindsay, formed a like contrast.[31] The cost of holding sessions of the legislature under the provisional government was $83,856.60 in 1865–1866, and $83,852 in 1866–1867. Under Smith it was about $90,000 per session, and there were three regular sessions the first year. One session (1870–1871) under Lindsay cost $95,442.30, and two under Lewis, 1873–1874, cost $175,661.50 and $166,602.65 respectively.[32] The cost of keeping state prisoners for trial was about $50,000 a year. The Reconstruction legislature cut down expenses by passing a law to liberate criminals of a grade below that of felon, upon their own recognizance.[33]

The Democrats complained of the way the reconstructionists spent the contingent fund of the state. This abuse was never so bad as in other southern states at the time, but still there was continual stealing on a small scale. Some examples[34] may be given: Governor Lewis spent $800 on a short visit to New York and Florida;[35] the governor's private secretary received $21,000 for services rendered in distributing the "political" bacon in 1874;[36] the treasurer drew $1200 to pay

Montgomery Mail, Dec. 31, 1870. There were about 10 in 1900.

[29] Journal of the "Capitol" Senate, 1872, pp. 19–34; in Senate Journal, 1873.

[30] The older and abler men were disfranchised.

[31] *Montgomery Mail,* Sept. 22, 1872.

[32] Auditor's Reports, 1869–1873.

[33] The purpose of the act was to liberate negro prisoners and save money for the officials to spend in other ways.

[34] These items are taken from the accounts of Lewis's administration.

[35] The Investigating Committee remarked that had he chartered a parlor car and paid hotel bills at the rate of $10 a day, he would have been unable to spend $800 on that trip.

[36] See Ch. XXIV.

his expenses to Mobile and New York, though he had no business to attend to in either place, and travelled on roads over which he had passes; ex-Governor W. H. Smith, when attorney for the Alabama and Chattanooga Railroad, was paid $500 by the state for services rendered in connection with his own road, and the committee was unable to discover the nature of these services; the secretary of state charged $952 for signing his name to bonds, though it was his constitutional duty to do so without charge; a bill of stationery from Benedict of New York cost $7761.58, when the bid of Joel White of Montgomery on the same order was $4336.54; $50 was allowed to John A. Bingham (presumably a relative of the treasurer) for signing enough bonds to purchase a farm for the penitentiary. Such purchases as these were common: one refrigerator, $65; one looking-glass, $5; one clothes-brush, $1.50. Very few of the small accounts against the contingent fund were itemized. In no case were any of them accounted for by proper vouchers. The private secretary of the governor was in the habit of approving and allowing accounts against the contingent fund, even going so far as to approve the governor's own accounts. The Investigating Committee said that the private secretary seemed to be the acting governor.[37]

The Florida commissioners, J. L. Pennington, C. A. Miller, and A. J. Walker, who were appointed to negotiate for the cession to Alabama of West Florida, spent $10,500, of which Walker, the Democratic member, spent $516, and Miller and Pennington spent the remainder, "according to the best judgment and discretion" of themselves. They claimed that part of it was used to entertain the Florida commissioners, and part to influence the elections in West Florida.[38]

The governor was accused of transferring appropriations. In one case, he drew out of the treasury $484,346.76, ostensibly to pay the interest on the public debt, and used it for other purposes. A committee appointed to investigate was able to trace all of it except $75,196.56, which sum could not be accounted for. The accounts were carelessly kept. The auditor, treasurer, and governor never seemed to know within a million or two of dollars what the public debt was. The reports for the period from 1868 to 1875 do not show the actual condition of the finances, and the Debt Commission in 1875 was unable to get accurate information from the state records, but had to advertise for information from the creditors and debtors of the state.[39]

Effect on Property Values

The misrule of the Radicals in Alabama resulted in a general shrinkage in values after 1867, especially in the Black Belt, where financial and economic chaos reigned supreme, and where the carpetbagger flourished supported by the negro votes. Recuperation was impossible until the rule of the alien was overthrown. This was done in some of the white counties in 1870. At that date land values were still 60 per cent below those of 1860, and the numbers of live stock 40 per cent below. This was due largely to

---

[37] Report of the Committee to Investigate the Contingent Fund, 1875; Senate Journal, 1874–1875, pp. 581–607.

[38] Caffey, "The Annexation of West Florida to Alabama," p. 10; Senate Journal, 1869–1870, pp. 234–244.

[39] Report of the Committee to examine the Offices of Auditor and Treasurer, 1875; Report of the Debt Commission, 1875, 1876.

the condition of the Black Belt counties under the control of the Radicals.[40]

Thousands of landowners were unable to pay the taxes assessed, and their farms were sold by the state. The *Independent Monitor*, on March 8, 1870, advertised the sale of 1284 different lots of land (none less than forty acres) in Tuscaloosa County, and the next week 2548 more were advertised for sale, all to pay taxes. Often, it was complained, the tax assessor failed to notify the people to "give in" their taxes, and thus caused them trouble. In some cases, where costs and fines were added to the original taxes, it amounted to confiscation. In 1871, F. S. Lyon exhibited before the Ku Klux Committee a copy of the *Southern Republican* containing twenty-one and a half columns of advertised sales of land lying in the rich counties of Marengo, Greene, Perry, and Choctaw.[41] One Radical declared that he wanted the taxes raised so high that the large landholders would be compelled to sell their lands, so that he, and others like him, could buy.[42] Property sold for taxes could be redeemed only by paying double the amount of the taxes plus the costs. A tax sale deed was conclusive evidence of legal sale, and was not a subject for the decision of a court.[43]

There were hundreds of mortgage sales in every county of the state during the Reconstruction period. At these sales everything from land to household furniture was sold. The court-house squares on sale days were favorite gathering places for the negroes, who came to look on, and a traveller, in 1874, states that in the immense crowds of negroes at the sales there were some who had come a distance of sixty miles.[44] Each winter, from 1869 to 1875, there was an exodus of people to Texas and to South America, driven from their homes by mortgages, taxes, the condition of labor, and corrupt government. Landowners sold their lands for what they would bring and went to the West, where there were no negroes, no scalawags, and no carpet-baggers.[45]

Most of the farmers and tenants of that period were unable to send their children to school and pay tuition. The reconstructed school system failed almost at the beginning. Consequently, tens of thousands of children grew up ignorant of schools, most of them the children of parents who had had some education. Hence the special provision for them in the constitution of 1901. The first Democratic legislature restricted taxation to three-fifths of one per cent and local taxation to one-half of one per cent. The rates were lowered gradually, until in the early nineties the rate was only two-fifths of one per cent. Since that time, the rate has again increased until in 1899 the state tax was again three-fourths of one per cent, the increase being used for Confederate pensions and for schools.

---

40 See Edwin DeLeon, "Ruin and Reconstruction of the Southern States," in the *Southern Magazine*, Jan., 1874.

41 Ala. Test., p. 1409.

42 State Journal, April 19, 1874.

43 Ala. Test., p. 1409. The Radical newspapers that had the public printing made money from the tax sale notices by dividing each lot into sixteenths of a section, advertising each, and charging for each division. The author of the tax sale law was Pierce Burton, a Radical editor.

44 *Scribner's Monthly*, Aug., 1874; King, "The Great South."

45 *Southern Argus*, Jan. 17 and Feb. 8, 1872; *Scribner's Monthly*, Aug., 1874; Herbert, "Solid South," pp. 64, 67. Colonel Herbert believes that during the six years of Reconstruction the state gained practically nothing by immigration, while it lost more by emigration than it had by the Civil War.

But in addition to the expenditure of the sums raised by extraordinary taxation, the Reconstruction administration greatly increased the bonded debt of the state and by mortgaging the future left a heavy burden upon the people that has as yet been but slightly lessened.

The Public Bonded Debt

After 1868 it is impossible to ascertain what the public debt of the state was at any given time until 1875, when the first Democratic legislature began to investigate the condition of the finances.

In 1860 the total debt — state bonds and trust funds — was $5,939,654.87 (and the bonded debt was $3,445,000), most of which was due to the failure of the state bank. The payment of the war debt, which amounted to $13,094,732.95, was forbidden by the Fourteenth Amendment. In 1865 the total bonded debt with three years' unpaid interest was $4,065,410, while the trust funds amounted to $2,910,000. Governor Patton reissued the bonds to the amount of $4,087,800, and the sixteenth section and the university trust funds with unpaid interest raised the total debt, in 1867, to $6,130,910. In July, 1868, when the state went into the hands of the reconstructionists, the total debt was $6,848,400. The provisional government had been increasing the debt because no taxes were collected during 1865 and 1866. Taxes were collected in 1867, but before the end of 1868 the debt amounted to $7,904,398.92, and after that date no one knew, nor did the officials seem to care, exactly how large it was.[46]

State and county and town bonds were issued in reckless haste by the plunderers,

[46] Auditor's Reports, 1869–1873; Comptroller's Reports, 1861–1865, 1866; Patton's Report, 1867, to the Convention; Journal Convention of 1867, pp. 46, 123; Ku Klux Rept., pp. 169, 317, 1055.

but the reports do not show the amounts issued; no correct records were kept. The acts of the legislature authorized the governor to issue about $5,000,000 state bonds, besides the direct bonds issued to railroads, which amounted to about $4,000,000 not including interest. The counties, besides being authorized to levy heavy additional taxes, were permitted to issue bonds for various purposes.[47] A number of acts gave the counties general permission to issue bonds, but there are no records accessible of the amounts

[47] The following is a partial list compiled from the session laws: —

Issues of County Bonds

1868.	Walker County	$14,000.00
1868.	Dallas County	50,000.00
1868.	Bullock County	40,000.00
1868.	Limestone County	100,000.00
1868.	Hale County	60,000.00
1869.	Greene County	80,000.00
1869.	Pickens County	100,000.00
1870.	Baldwin County	5,000.00
1870.	Bibb County	5,000.00
1870.	Choctaw County	(?)unlimited
1870.	Crenshaw County	10,000.00
1872.	Pickens County	30,000.00
1873.	Butler County	12,000.00
1873.	Jefferson County	50,000.00
1873.	Montgomery County	130,000.00
1873.	Madison County	130,000.00
(?)	Dallas County	140,000.00
(?)	Chambers County	150,000.00
(?)	Lee County	275,000.00
(?)	Randolph County	100,000.00
(?)	Barbour County	(?)
(?)	Tallapoosa County	125,000.00

Issues of Town and City Bonds

1868.	Troy	$75,000.00
1869.	Eutaw	20,000.00
1869.	Greensboro	15,000.00
1871.	Mobile	1,400,000.00
1871.	Selma	500,000.00
1872.	Prattville	50,000.00
1873.	Mobile	200,000.00
(?)	Opelika	25,000.00

And in addition each county and town had a large floating debt in "scrip" or local obligations. Speculators gathered up such obligations and sold them at reduced prices to those who had local taxes, fines, and licenses to pay.

raised. There were issues of town and county bonds without legislative authorization. This practice is said to have been common, but in the chaotic conditions of the time little attention was paid to such things and no records were kept.

To dispose of its bonds the state had a large number of financial agents in the North and abroad. Some of these made no reports at all; others reported as they pleased. Certain bonds were sold in 1870 by one of the financial agents, and two years later the proceeds had not reached the treasury or been accounted for. In like manner some bond sales were conducted in 1871 and in 1872.[48] Not only was no record kept of the issues of direct and indorsed bonds, but no records were kept of the payment of interest and of the domestic debts of the state. Some of the financial agents exercised the authority of auditor and treasurer and settled any claim that might be presented to them. Some agents, who paid interest on bonds, returned the cancelled coupons; others did not. In Governor Lewis's office $20,000 in coupons were found with nothing to show that they had been cancelled. One lot of bonds was received with every coupon attached, yet the interest on these had been paid regularly in New York.[49]

Provision was made for the retirement of all "state money"; but if the treasury was empty when it came in, it was apt to be reissued without any authority of law. A large sum was returned, but no record was made of it, and it was not destroyed. Later it was discovered among a mass of waste paper, where any thief might have taken it and put it again into circulation. One transaction may be cited as an illustration of the management of the finances: in 1873 the state owed Henry Clews & Company $299,660.20. Governor Lewis gave his notes (twelve in number) as governor, for the amount, and at the same time deposited with Clews as collateral security $650,000 in state bonds. Clews, when he failed, turned over the governor's notes to the Fourth National Bank of New York, to which he was indebted. He had already disposed of, so the state claimed, the $650,000 in bonds which he held as collateral security; and a year later, according to the Debt Commission, he still made a claim against the state for $235,039.43 as a balance due him. Thus a debt of $299,660.20 had grown in the hands of one of the state agents to $1,184,689.63, besides interest.[50]

In 1872 it was estimated that the general liabilities of the state, counties, and towns amounted to $52,762,000.[51] The country was flooded with temporary obligations receivable for public dues, and the tax collectors substituted these for any coin that might come into their hands. There was much speculation in the depreciated currency by the state and county officials. During Lewis's first year (1873), the state bonds were quoted at

[48] Auditor's Reports, 1871–1872; Report of Committee on Public Debt, 1876; McClure, "The South: Industrial, Financial, and Political Condition," p. 83.

[49] Report of the Committee on Public Debt, 1876; Senate Journal, 1872–1873, p. 544; Auditor's Report, 1873.

[50] Senate Journal, 1875–1876, pp. 212, 213; Report of the Committee on the Public Debt, 1876. In his book Clews tells how he invested in the securities of the struggling southern states, being desirous of assisting them. But when the ungrateful states refused to pay the claims that he and others like him presented, he says it was because they, the creditors, were northern men. See Clews, "Twenty-eight Years in Wall Street," pp. 550, 551.

[51] DeLeon, "Ruin and Reconstruction," in the *Southern Magazine*, Jan., 1874. The state debts of the ten southern states were then estimated at $291,626,015, while the debts of the other twenty-seven states amounted to only $293,-872,552.

60 per cent, but on November 17, 1873, he reported, "This department has been unable to sell for money any of the state bonds during the present administration." He raised money for immediate needs by hypothecation of the state securities. Thus came about the remarkable trans-

action with Clews. The state money went down to 60 per cent, then to 40 per cent before the elections of 1874, and at one time state bonds sold for cash at 20 and 21 cents on the dollar.[52]

52 Houston's Message, 1876; Senate Journal, 1874–1875, p. 7.

Horace Mann Bond:

SOCIAL AND ECONOMIC FORCES IN ALABAMA RECONSTRUCTION

THE story of Reconstruction in Alabama, more than a twice-told tale, has become a commonly accepted pattern for the historical description of the South. In the definitive work of Walter Lynwood Fleming,[1] the central figures and facts are set forth with a conviction, and documentation, that for thirty years has closed the subject to further investigation.

The central figures in this stereotype are the shiftless, poor white scalawags; the greedy carpetbaggers; the ignorant, deluded, sometimes vicious Negroes; and the noble, courageous and chivalrous Southrons who fought and won the battle for White Supremacy. The accepted facts are: the imposition of a corrupt carpetbagger-Negro régime on a proud State; the accumulation of a debt· of $25,503,593;[2] the final victory of Hon-

esty; and the shouldering of this immense debt by a war-ridden, despoiled people who toiled for generations under the incubus of fearful interest payments.

We enjoy, today, an advantage in perspective over Fleming, who was himself the son of a planter partially ruined by the War, and whose thesis, in some degree, was the expression of a class-attitude affected by the events of the Civil War and Reconstruction, thinking in terms of ethical evaluations, and seeking, as even historians will, to fix blame. It is pertinent to remember that Fleming wrote, and published, less than thirty years after the occurrence of the events he described.

There is precedent for linking the long-favored figures of the Reconstruction history to the less romantic forces by which

1 Civil War and Reconstruction in Alabama. New York: The Columbia University Press (Macmillan), 1905.

2 In Black Reconstruction (New York: Harcourt,

Brace and Co., 1935), W. E. B. Du Bois hints at a re-examination of the nature of the Alabama debt. However, he gives Fleming's figure as bona-fide for 1874, and makes no later correction of this as a final figure for the Alabama debt.

Reprinted from Horace Mann Bond, "Social and Economic Forces in Alabama Reconstruction," Journal of Negro History, XXIII (July, 1938), 290, 310, 313–326, 330–348.

". . . the planting class was being trampled in the dust — stripped of its wealth and political power —(while)— the capitalist class was marching onward in seven league boots."[3] With an eye to what happened in Alabama, Russ says that the process of disfranchisement in the South "played an important part in producing modern Industrial America," through keeping the "ex-leaders of the South" out of Congress until it was too late to change the new industrial order which had become firmly entrenched in the interim."[4] Whether these grand motives affected policy in Alabama, so far as internal politics was concerned, may be doubted.

What is doubtless is the value of the point of view for interpreting the record of Reconstruction in Alabama, for Alabama was more likely to witness the working of unsuspected economic forces than any other Southern state. Its natural resources were unique in the South; and, in an age when Coal was power, and Iron the other necessity for industry, it was already known that the Northern hill-country of Alabama had both in unexampled proximity. The bankers in Philadelphia and New York, and even in London, and Paris, had known this for almost two decades. The only thing lacking was transportation.

We propose to examine here the thesis, that the most important elements involved in the Reconstruction of Alabama were the economic factors incident to the State itself and to the times. . . .

Capital in Alabama — Railroads, Coal, and Iron. In 1850 the "Little Giant,"

Stephen A. Douglas, visited Alabama, spending most of the time in Mobile. The result of his visit was eminently successful; the Alabama Congressional delegation, which in 1848 had been unanimously opposed to the Railroad Bill of that year as introduced by Douglas, in 1850 furnished the small majority by which it became law.[5] One reason for the change was that the 1850 bill made possible, with later enactments, a grant of 3,077,373 acres to various Alabama roads, in a compromise addition to the terms of the 1848 bill which specified a grant to the Illinois Central. The Alabama roads thus favored were the Mobile and Ohio, planned to make a juncture with the Illinois Central at Cairo; the Selma, Rome, and Dalton; the Alabama and Chattanooga; the South and North Alabama; and the Mobile and Girard.[6]

In 1852 a young man named Jabez Lamar Monroe Curry "traversed the counties of Talladega, Calhoun, and Randolph, making speeches, and obtaining rights of way and subscriptions" for the Alabama and Tennessee River Railroad Company, in which his father was a prominent stockholder.[7] In 1853 this young man was elected to the State Legislature from Talladega county, and was immediately appointed Chairman of the Committee on Internal Improvements.[8] He held membership also on the Committee on Education. Curry sponsored legislation to give state aid to rail-

---

3 Charles A. and Mary Beard, *The Rise of American Civilization*, II, p. 105.

4 William A. Russ, Jr., "Registration and Disfranchisement under Radical Reconstruction," *The Mississippi Valley Historical Review*, Vol. XII, No. 2, p. 180.

5 William Elejius Martin, *Internal Improvements in Alabama*, pp. 66–67. Johns Hopkins Studies in Historical and Political Science, Baltimore: Johns Hopkins Press, 1902.

6 William Elejius Martin, *Internal Improvements in Alabama*, p. 68.

7 E. A. Alderman and A. C. Gordon, *J. L. M. Curry, A Biography*, p. 105. New York: Macmillan Co., 1911. This road later merged with the Selma, Rome, and Dalton.

8 *Ibid.*, p. 105.

roads from his Committee on Internal Improvements.[9] Two measures which had more relationship than one might imagine were also sponsored by Curry; one became the basis for the foundation of the first public school system in Alabama, and the second authorized the appointment of a State Geologist whose duty it was to survey "the mineral resources, their location, and the best means for their development" in the interests of the State of Alabama.[10]

A fellow member of the legislature of 1853–1854 was one Luke Pryor, who had been elected from Madison County. He was "pledged to the work of securing authority to subscribe two hundred thousand dollars to the capital stock of the Tennessee and Alabama Central Railroad, at Nashville and Decatur, and secured the bill raising that tax, enacted over the veto of Governor Winston."[11] Curry's biographers give him the same credit; "his influence in the legislature, *or other undisclosed causes,* served to pass the State aid bills over the Governor's vetoes."[12]

The power behind Luke Pryor was James W. Sloss, described by Armes as Pryor's "side partner in railroad and commercial ventures."[13] Sloss's name is unheralded and unsung in the more romantic annals of Alabama Reconstruction, and yet his influence, on close inspection, will be found connected with every important industrial and commercial enterprise in the State during the latter half of the nineteenth century. Like Curry's father,[14] Sloss had accumulated capital

for investment in railroads, not from planting, but from store-keeping.[15] If the ventures of men like Sloss were less spectacular than those of the great planters of the Black Belt, and of his own Tennessee Valley; and if they are less known to history, it is because this was the Southern version of the new class of capitalists and industrialists, manipulating great affairs of State in the obscurity of public inattention while public officials basked in the outward gaze of the multitude.

In 1855 Sloss was president of the Tennessee and Alabama Central Railroad, and it was for this line that Luke Pryor "was sent to the State Legislature."[16] Meanwhile, some five hundred miles to the North of Sloss's smaller principality, James Guthrie, President of the Louisville and Nashville Railroad, "was establishing that road as the political control of the State" of Kentucky.[17] The L. & N. early had visions of extending its empire to the South,[18] and James Sloss's enterprise in Alabama stretched northward toward Nashville, in the same direction which expansion for the L. & N. would, of necessity, involve. It was, perhaps, no accident that James Guthrie, President of the L. & N., in 1860, came into bitter conflict with the supporters of the "Little Giant" at the Charleston Convention.[19] In 1860 the candidate for a presidential nomination was still the former protagonist of the Illinois Central

[9] *Ibid.,* p. 106.
[10] *Ibid.,* p. 107.
[11] Owens, *Biography of Alabama,* IV, p. 1396.
[12] Alderman and Gordon, *op. cit.,* p. 106.
[13] Armes, *The Story of Coal and Iron,* p. 107.
[14] Alderman and Gordon, *op. cit.,* pp. 40–42, 108.

[15] Owens, *Biography of Alabama,* IV, 1572–1753.

[16] Armes, *op. cit.,* p. 107.

[17] George F. Milton, *The Eve of Conflict,* p. 403. Cambridge: The Riverside Press, Houghton, Mifflin and Co., 1935.

[18] Ellis Merton Coulter, *The Cincinnati Southern Railroad and the Struggle for Southern Commerce, 1865–1872,* p. 7. Reprinted from *A History of Kentucky.* Chicago: American Historical Society, 1922.

[19] Milton, *op. cit.,* p. 374.

and the Mobile and Ohio Railroads. Could the feud, even thus early, have involved the ultimate goal of tapping Alabama's mineral wealth?

The Civil War left Alabama's railroads in poor condition; rolling stock, tracks, bridges, and other equipment were indiscriminately destroyed by contending armies in the ebb and flow of the tide of battle. Such disaster, however, does not seem to have overcome the fortunes of the North Alabama capitalists and politicians who were the associates of James Sloss. Robert Patton, a member of the Sloss North Alabama coterie, had a brother-in-law, J. J. Griers, who was in constant communication with General Grant during the War.[20] Patton was later Provisional Governor under the short-lived Johnson régime, and during his tenure of office worked in close cooperation with the Sloss interests.[21] George Houston, who became Luke Pryor's law partner in 1866,[22] had a most uncertain record of loyalty to the Confederacy.[23] Samuel Noble, later associated with Sloss in developing the mineral resources of North Alabama, and an ally of William

"Pig-Iron" Kelley,[24] traded through the lines with the connivance of Confederate and Federal officials.[25]

The Louisville and Nashville Railroad also emerged from the war with enhanced prospects. As the direct carrier between North and South of the immense Federal business, the line had extraordinary profits during the War,[26] and its "wonderful prosperity" then attained continued until 1870.[27] By the end of the War Sloss's railroad interests were already inextricably bound up with the L. & N. In 1865 three small roads in North Alabama, including the Tennessee and Alabama, combined under Sloss's leadership.[28] In 1866 Albert Fink, General Superintendent of the L. & N., spoke in his Report to the Directors as though the Sloss roads were already a part of the L. & N. system, as, indeed, they probably were.

. . . *Decatur and Montgomery Railroad.* This road, when completed, will, by connecting Decatur with Montgomery, Alabama, form a most important link, in the through line from Louisville, to Montgomery, Mobile and Pensacola, and open to the enterprise of Louisville the rich country tributary to the above cities.[29]

---

[20] *O.R.R.* Ser. I. Vol. XLIX, Pt. 1, pp. 590, 718; Pt. II, p. 560; Fleming, *Civil War and Reconstruction*, p. 146.

[21] The Patton Government began the convict lease system in 1866 with a lease to James W. Sloss and others. (*First Biennial Report of the Inspectors of Convicts*, containing reprints of special message by Rufus W. Cobb, Governor, dated November 27, 1882. Montgomery: Barrett & Co., 1886.) Patton served as Vice-President of the Alabama and Chattanooga Railroad in 1869–1870 while this road was still partially under the control of the Sloss interests (*Poor's Manual, 1869–1870,* p. 420.) The Tennessee and Alabama Central, a Sloss affiliate, held a mortgage on the Alabama and Chattanooga during this period. (Armes, *The Story of Coal and Iron,* p. 216.)

[22] Owens, *Biography of Alabama,* IV, p. 1396.

[23] Fleming, *Civil War and Reconstruction,* pp. 190–195.

[24] "Pig-Iron" Kelley's first visit to Alabama in 1867 was to view the mineral resources of North Alabama and to make speeches for Republican Reconstruction. In Mobile one of his speeches to Negroes precipitated a race riot. In 1885 he revisited the State and published a brief book, *The Old South and the New* (New York: G. P. Putnam's Sons, 1888) giving his impressions. Kelley was financially interested in Samuel Noble's iron works at Anniston. His second impressions were bucolically peaceful. He was an adherent of Booker T. Washington and favored the Industrial Education of Negroes.

[25] Fleming, *op. cit.,* p. 194.

[26] *Affairs of Southern Railroads,* p. 622.

[27] Coulter, *The Cincinnati Southern,* p. 11.

[28] *Affairs of Southern Railroads,* p. 697.

[29] *Ibid.*

By 1867 the L. & N. had come to terms with the Mobile and Ohio, negotiating a ten-year lease of the property.[30] But at Nashville the L. & N. found a strong competitor for the Alabama mineral regions' trade, in the Nashville and Chattanooga.[31] The struggle between the competing interests may be simplified as follows: Should the L. & N. affiliates, by way of the Nashville and Decatur (later the North and South Railroad) have access to Alabama's coal and iron, or should the Nashville and Chattanooga, and its controlling capitalists, win the field through extending a line from Chattanooga to the southwestward along the Tennessee River Valley?

Railroads and Reconstruction: First Phase: Officially, in the public eye and that of later historians, the actors in this dramatic struggle were, respectively, Republicans and Democrats, fighting for the slogan of "White Supremacy," on the one hand, or "Equal Rights" on the other. Not apparent on the political stage, but working powerfully behind the scenes, were such men as James Guthrie, Albert Fink, and James Sloss of the L. & N.; and V. K. Stevenson, the principal apparent owner of the Nashville and Chattanooga.[32] These men in turn had their masters. A local, but not altogether a minor capitalist, was Josiah Morris, a Montgomery banker, who is listed as a large stockholder and a director of all the Sloss railroad affiliates.[33]

V. K. Stevenson is said to have been supported by "Boston Financiers," made visible in the person of Russell Sage.[34] The L. & N. was financed largely by local Louisville capital, with frequent and sizable contributions from the municipality itself. The name of August Belmont — and this suggests, not only the activity of the Chairman of the National Democratic Party, but also of the omnipresent and almost omnipotent Rothschilds, of whom he was the American agent,[35] — was also linked to the financing of the L. & N., especially in enterprises connected with the opening of Alabama coal fields.[36]

Sam Tate, a prominent figure in Tennessee railroad building and politics, was also a factor in Alabama.[37] Tate was the builder and president of the Memphis and Charleston, a road traversing North Alabama from the Mississippi line, on the West, running just South of the Tennessee River to Decatur, where a bridge had been built, and terminating at Stevenson, with a connecting line from that point to Chattanooga.[38] Like Albert Fink, of the L. & N., Tate had the same vision of the possibilities of exploiting Alabama's mineral resources:

Decatur to Montgomery is another important connection, feeding your entire line with shares as the result of a loan to Colonel F. M. Gilmer, who deposited the stock as collateral, and could not repay the loan. He was a private banker. He was a calm, and unemotional old man. He was in no sense a developer, as the term is nowadays used. He did not build towns, or railroads, nor factories; but his millions strengthened the confidence of the public."

---

[30] Coulter, *The Cincinnati Southern*, p. 8; *Poor's Manual, 1870–1871*, p. 267.

[31] *Affairs of Southern Railroads*, p. 623.

[32] Armes, *op. cit.*, p. 243.

[33] Morris died March 18, 1891, at Montgomery. The following newspaper account appeared at that time in the *Birmingham Age-Herald*: "He was the richest man in Alabama. . . . He held 660 shares of the 2,000 of the Elyton Land Company, which in 1874 sold for $17 a share. At his death they were valued at $4,000 a share. He got many

[34] Armes, *op. cit.*, p. 243.

[35] Herbert L. Casson, *The Romance of Steel*, p. 301. New York: A. S. Barnes and Co., 1907.

[36] *Ibid.*

[37] James Phelan, *History of Tennessee, the Making of a State*, pp. 284–290. Boston and New York: Houghton Mifflin Co., 1889.

[38] *Affairs of Southern Railroads*, p. 723.

an abundance of iron and coal, with seventy-five miles of your line from which tonnage for local consumption would alone be profitable, to say nothing of the immense amount of western produce you would carry over your lines to feed the thousands of operatives that will be employed in developing the vast resources of mineral wealth in the mountains south of Decatur. Your fostering aid and care should be extended to this road, too, as early as practicable, as it will be one of its most productive arteries.[39]

Indeed, at this time (1866) a close cooperation was in effect between the L. & N., represented by Fink, and the Memphis and Charleston, as represented by Tate. Fink rebuilt the bridge for the Memphis and Charleston at Decatur which had been destroyed during the War.[40] Tate got the contract for building the road he and Fink had proposed.[41]

By act of February 19, 1867, the General Assembly of Alabama embarked on the adventure of giving the State endorsement to railroad bonds of certain extant companies,[42] in the amount of $12,000 a mile. This legislation was enacted in the face of impending congressional reconstruction. This was the Provisional Assembly, with Governor Robert Patton, North Alabamian, and associate of Sloss, in control; and the endorsements included only those roads which were controlled by the coterie associated with Sloss. The South and North, the Montgomery and Eufaula, the Montgomery and Mobile, the Northeast and the Southwest, and the Wills Valley Roads were

the beneficiaries.[43] An examination of the directorates of these railroads will show the presence of Sloss, of Pryor, of Houston, of Morris; i.e., the leading politico-capitalists who figured in the Democratic (Conservative) Party during Reconstruction.[44]

When a Republican General Assembly was convened on July 13, 1868 — the work of railroad endorsement had been done hurriedly in the waning days of the Provisional Assembly, when pending bills in Congress assured Republican control by the next year — a brief period ensued during which strange industrial and capitalistic bedfellows made political peace for mutual profit.

The Wills Valley and the Northeast and Northwest roads were combined and incorporated as the Alabama and Chattanooga. The formal date of the merger was October 6, 1868.[45] In a series of acts of the General Assembly during the session of 1868–1869, the State endorsement for railroad bonds was increased from $12,000 to $16,000 a mile.[46] The increased endorsement was not a "Republican" grab; for a brief period Sloss enjoyed a paramount interest in the South and North, and the Alabama and Chattanooga, which became the particular beneficiaries of the raised endorsement. Robert Patton, his associate in politics and business, and formerly Governor under the Provisional Government, became a Vice President of the new Alabama and Chattanooga road, whose bonds he had aided in endorsing shortly

39 *Ibid.*

40 *Ibid.*, p. 722.

41 Armes, *op. cit.*, pp. 246–247.

42 George E. Houston, "Message of the Governor, including Report of the Commissioners on the Public Debt," *Journal of the House of Representatives,* 1875–1876, p. 209. W. W. Screws and Co., 1876.

43 Fleming, *op. cit.*, p. 591.

44 See *Affairs of Southern Railroads,* and *Poor's Manual* for the years indicated, for lists of directors and officials.

45 *Poor's Manual, 1868–1869,* pp. 419–421.

46 *Ku Klux Conspiracy, Alabama Testimony,* pp. 193–199, 359–361, 1056, 1058, 1411, 1417–1418.

before as Governor.[47] John T. Milner, Engineer of the South and North, and John C. Stanton, who held a like responsibility with the Alabama and Chattanooga, joined in bribing members of the Assembly. A history of industrialization in Alabama, bearing the official approval of the Birmingham Chamber of Commerce, has this account of the manner in which the finances of the South and North were rescued under Republican rule.

Mr. John T. Milner, Engineer of the Road, said that John Whiting, a Montgomery cotton factor, President of the South and North Railroad, told him "he spurned the idea of getting among these Yankees at all, much less of paying them for their votes," but he said that "I might do so if I felt like it. So I went."[48]

Milner's ventures were financed principally by Josiah Morris, the Montgomery banker. Stanton was the field agent of Russell Sage. The South and North, as an extension of the main line of the Louisville and Nashville, through 1868–1869 apparently had a working agreement with the Alabama and Chattanooga, through which the two lines were to be connected at a strategic point in the mineral region where a great industrial city would be built. The legislators were

generous both with the South and North, planned to run from Montgomery to Decatur and there to connect with the L. & N., and with the Alabama and Chattanooga, which was planned to run from Chattanooga across the state to Meridian, and from there, eventually, to New Orleans. In 1868 the South and North received the 2 and 3 per cent funds as a loan from the State.[49] By February 5, 1870, the Alabama and Chattanooga was loaned $2,000,000 by the State.[50]

A recounting of the liabilities assumed for these two railroad systems shows that between 1867 and 1871 — under, first, a Provisional, "Conservative" government, and, later, under a "Radical" Republican government — the State incurred what have been called *debts* of approximately $17,000,000 in endorsements and loans. Of this amount L. & N. affiliates (the South and North, the Montgomery and Eufaula, etc.) accounted for $7,000,000; while obligations assumed for the Alabama and Chattanooga, and railroads represented in this merger, equalled approximately $10,000,000.[51] Since the Alabama "debt" at the end of Reconstruction has been estimated at a maximum of $30,000,000, and $9,000,000 represented ante-Reconstruction obligations, it is ob-

[47] *Poor's Manual, 1870–1871,* p. 104. In 1866 Patton, as provisional Governor, began the Alabama convict lease system in a contract signed with a Mr. Smith and a Mr. McMillan. Subsequently, it was shown that these men were "dummies" for a group which included James W. Sloss and Sam Tate. The convicts were used first for railroad construction, and the highly lucrative, however iniquitous, system of lease to coal mines and foundries followed shortly thereafter. (*First Biennial Report of the Inspectors of Convicts to the Governor, from October 1, 1884–October 1, 1886,* p. 352. Montgomery: Barrett & Co., 1886.) Incidentally, it is interesting to note that a Captain John H. Bankhead was one of the first official

figures in the new convict system. So much is made in the current press of the aristocratic antecedents of the Bankhead family (great planters, hundreds of slaves, etc., etc.) that it would probably be indelicate to expand here the speculation that at least a considerable portion of the Bankhead fortune was founded on the beginning of the convict lease system in Alabama, *after the Civil War;* and that the political as well as economic great-god-father of the present Senator and Congressman was none other than unsung James W. Sloss of North Alabama.

[48] Armes, *op. cit.,* p. 216.

[49] Martin, *Internal Improvements in Alabama,* p. 71.

[50] Fleming, *op. cit.,* p. 593.

[51] George S. Houston, "Message of the Governor," *House Journal, 1875–1876,* pp. 187–217.

vious how largely the manipulations of these two railroad systems alone entered into the final financial picture of the period.[52]

The apparent co-operation of the two groups of capitalists — the L. & N. group, on the one hand, and the Alabama and Chattanooga (Russell Sage) on the other — came to an end in November, 1870. The Democratic candidate for Governor, Lindsay, was elected over his Republican opponent, with a Democratic lower House and a Republican hold-over Senate. An agreement had been reached between the sponsors of the lines financed by the Louisville and Nashville, and the Alabama and Chattanooga, to locate the crossing of the railroads at a certain site in Jefferson county. The Stanton brothers, of the Alabama and Chattanooga (agents for Russell Sage) had taken options on the land surrounding the proposed crossing.[53] A group of Alabama capitalists, including Josiah Morris, W. S. Mudd, F. M. Gilmer, James W. Sloss, and others, took options on a new site, and, unknown to the Stantons, changed the route of the South and North so that it intersected with the Alabama and Chattanooga through the area which they controlled.[54]

The triumph of the local capitalists threatened to be of but brief duration. V. K. Stevenson and Russell Sage had acquired a majority of the $2,200,000 worth of bonds issued by the state in endorsing the building of the South and North.[55] They now (1871) threatened to foreclose on their mortgage, demanding as an alternative that the South and

North, already constructed from Montgomery to the Alabama and Chattanooga crossing, be turned over to the latter railroad for operation.[56]

In this crisis Albert Fink, said already to have had an agreement with James Sloss, "and at all times a helper and co-operator, along with Luke Pryor[57] and George Houston,[58] of the South and North," met the backers of the L. & N. at a hastily convened conference in Louisville.[59] Perhaps ratifying a convention already in force, the L. & N. agreed to take open and complete control of the South and North, averted Russell Sage's threatened foreclosure, and dated the agreement as of May 19, 1871.[60]

The point of these inter-industrial feuds to our discussion is that they dominated every political maneuver that took place in the State during these troublous times. The Democratic and Republican Parties in Alabama, viewed from this angle, seem to have been only the obverse aspects of the L. & N. Railroad on the one hand, and the Alabama and Chattanooga Railroad on the other. The political tactics developed during this struggle was strikingly similar to contemporary developments in other states.

In Kentucky and Tennessee the L. & N. was said to "hide behind the City of Louisville" in its classic feud with Cincinnati. Promoters in the latter city proposed to build a road from Cincinnati to Chattanooga which would become the natural competitor of the L. & N.[61] Un-

52 *Poor's Manual for 1878–1879*, p. 993.

53 Armes, *op. cit.*, pp. 243–245.

54 *Ibid*. This was the nucleus of the Elyton Land Company, which, with the development of Birmingham, made such immense fortunes for those who were able to maintain their stock.

55 Armes, *op. cit.*, p. 243.

56 *Ibid.*

57 Later United States Senator from Alabama.

58 As the "Bald Eagle of the Mountains," Houston won the battle for "White Supremacy," in 1875, became Governor, and later United States Senator.

59 Armes, *op. cit.*, p. 245.

60 *Ibid.*

61 Coulter, *The Cincinnati Southern*, p. 28.

able to obtain capital elsewhere, the promoters managed to get a grant of $10,000,000 from the City of Cincinnati itself.[62] The L. & N. "ably supported Louisville in this fight," against the threatened competition from the sister city on the Ohio.[63] When proposed legislative aid to the Cincinnati-sponsored road was pending in the Kentucky legislature, ". . . it was claimed by the friends of the bill that this gigantic corporation (i.e., the L. & N.) was the main source of opposition, trying to hide behind the City (Louisville)."[64] The L. & N. adopted as its principal tactical weapon in Kentucky, identification with the political, social and ideological pattern of the stricken South. "Isaac Caldwell, who was one of Louisville's stanchest defenders, accused Cincinnati of helping to vote Negro suffrage upon Kentucky, and then immediately coming and asking a special favor for doing so."[65] Louisville (i.e., the L. & N.) hired merchants ". . . to go South and appeal to the disloyalty of their political record to seduce custom, and when they find that the South demands a better market than she affords, it again appeals to the more sectional feeling at home to prevent the South from getting to that market."[66] If there is any truth in this partisan accusation, it is the suggestion that capital — as represented by the L. & N. — preceded the politicians in appealing to racial and sectional interests. The fact that the L. & N. in Alabama was closely identified with local capitalists, while the Alabama and Chattanooga had such men as the "Stantons of Boston" in the chief place of prominence in operations there, is an important key to politics in the State during the crucial years of Reconstruction.

Industrial Conflict and Debt. 1871–1876: With this background, both political and industrial conflict in Alabama during the latter stages of Reconstruction becomes understandable. Reference has been made above to the close cooperation existing between the officials of the affiliated lines of the L. & N. in Alabama, and the Democratic administration elected in the fall of 1870. According to the terms of state endorsements, the State was liable for interest payments in the event of defaults by the roads. The Alabama and Chattanooga defaulted payment of interest due immediately after the new Democratic administration went into office, as of January 1, 1871.[67] Governor Lindsay did not take over the road at that time, stating that to do so would acknowledge the validity of the grants to the Road, which his faction rejected as the corrupt malpractice of the prior Republican administration. When the railroad made its second default in June, 1871 (two weeks after the Louisville and Nashville had contracted to take over the South and North), Lindsay had different advice from his supporters; and he seized the road for the State, and appointed Colonel Gindrat and James H. Clanton as receivers.[68] Clanton was, at the time, Chairman of the Democratic State Executive Committee.[69] He was also a director of the Montgomery and Eufaula Road,

[62] Coulter, *op. cit.*, pp. 32–34.
[63] *Ibid.*, p. 44.
[64] *Ibid.*
[65] *Ibid.*, p. 15.
[66] *Ibid.*

[67] *Journal of the House, 1870–1871*, p. 82.
[68] William H. Moore, *Report of the Commissioner to investigate and audit claims against the State of Alabama, on account of the Alabama and Chattanooga Railroad*, pp. 3–4. Montgomery: Arthur Bingham, State Printer, 1873. In the meantime, it will be remembered that the L. & N. had openly agreed to take over complete control of the South and North. See p. 325, above.
[69] *Ku Klux Conspiracy, Alabama Testimony*, p. 226.

soon to become officially an affiliate of the L. & N. system.[70] Among his fellow directors were Josiah Morris, of Montgomery, and Bolling Hall,[71] politician, director of the South and North, and one of the founders of the Elyton Land Company.

Clanton is frequently quoted in Fleming's work on Reconstruction as a paragon of pure political motive.[72] The Montgomery and Eufaula railroad, with the Alabama and Chattanooga, was a beneficiary of the extensive endorsements and State loans negotiated during the prior period.[73] In 1871 Clanton was killed in a brawl in Knoxville by one Nelson, who was employed by the Stanton, or Alabama and Chattanooga interests.[74] There is a certain irony in Fleming's eulogy of Clanton: "He was killed in Knoxville by a hireling of one of the railroad companies which had looted the state treasury and which he was fighting."[75]

The Alabama and Chattanooga dragged through a long period of litigation during the next few years. From July, 1871, to October, 1872, it was operated by the State.[76] The interest on the A. & C. bonds alone amounted to $500,000 a year.[77]

In 1872 David P. Lewis, Republican, was elected Governor of Alabama. Lewis immediately took steps to relieve the State of the devastating interest pay-

ments which had accumulated with successive defaults, following that of the Alabama and Chattanooga. By an agreement negotiated in the Spring of 1873, the railroad companies, through an Act known as the "$4,000 a mile law," agreed to turn in their $16,000-a-mile bonds, and to receive back $4,000-a-mile straight state bonds, thus reducing the State liability by 75 per cent.[78] In December of 1873, Governor Lewis stated that all of the roads involved had filed notice of their acceptance of the Act.[79]

It is strange that but little attention has been given to the effect of the Panic of 1873 upon the course of Reconstruction in the South. The failure of Jay Cooke removed from the scene, not only a heavy investor in Southern railroads, but also an "angel" of the Republican Party in the section; and left supreme in the field of these investments the combined forces of the Drexels and the rising Junius S. Morgan. While these circumstances may be of speculative interest here, they are worthy of study.

The majority of the Alabama and Chattanooga bonds had passed into the hands of a "group of English capitalists."[80] The accumulation of defaulted interest payments reached a peak in 1873, in the financial panic of that year. Even the L. & N. was completely prostrated. An operating deficit of $568,362 for the entire system in 1873 was laid at the doors of the South and North. "The prostration of the iron industries has greatly retarded the development of the rich mineral resources along the lines of that road, which had been greatly relied upon for

[70] *Poor's Manual, 1868*, p. 251.

[71] Owens, *op. cit.*, III, p. 726.

[72] Fleming, *op. cit.*, pp. 508, 512, 625, 630, 638.

[73] Houston, "Message of the Governor," *House Journal, 1875–1876*, pp. 187–217.

[74] William Garrett, *Reminiscences of Public Men in Alabama for Thirty Years*, pp. 632–645. Atlanta: Plantation Publishing Company's Press, 1872.

[75] Fleming, *op. cit.*, p. 508.

[76] Moore, *op. cit.*, p. 3.

[77] *House Journal, 1870–1871*, p. 82.

[78] *Commercial and Financial Chronicle*, May 17, 1873, Vol. XVI, No. 11, p. 659; December 13, 1873, Vol. XVII, No. 442, p. 803.

[79] *Ibid.*, p. 180.

[80] *Commercial and Financial Chronicle*, Vol. XVI, No. 398.

supplying it with a profitable business."[81] The result was that the L. & N. went into bankruptcy and the ownership of the line passed finally and completely from whatever local capitalists had shared in its major control before, into the hands of Eastern and European bankers.

The financial crisis made the election of 1874 of paramount importance to the persons involved, who saw an opportunity to rescue from the general wreckage whatever salvage might be had. Industrial conflict, accordingly, was sharply focussed in political conflict. The strictly racial and sectional interpretation of the period by Fleming is likely to suggest that all of the corruption visible in Alabama was an outcome of Black Republican thievery.[82] We may say that the basic economic issue of the campaign of 1874 in Alabama was to determine which of the financial interests involved would be able to make the best possible settlement with a state government bankrupted by the earnest efforts of both. Certain facts add piquancy to the general notion that Reconstruction in Alabama was a tightly drawn struggle between Virtue, as represented by the Democrats, and Vice, as represented by the Republicans.

Henry Clews, an associate of Jay Cooke, and a heavy investor in Southern issues, was among the most prominent of the bankers holding the Alabama railroad bonds which lay in the scale of battle.[83] Clews boasted of having negotiated Dix's nomination as Governor of New York, which, he believed, made Grant's renomination certain.[84] His interest in Alabama,

he said, was motivated by a noble-hearted impulse "to help the South and to help develop its resources."[85] He added, almost as an after-thought, that he had considered Alabama as the most profitable place for investment on account of its manifest industrial advantages over the North in the years immediately after the War.[86] Writing of the "repudiation" of Alabama issues owned by him, after the final victory of the Democrats, he laid it to "political manipulation."[87] In addition to investments in State issues, Clews was associated with Samuel Noble and William D. "Pig-Iron" Kelley in financing the Oxford Iron Works at Anniston, which lay along the right-of-way of the Alabama and Chattanooga, and was a director of the Selma and Gulf Railroad (projected to run from Selma to Pensacola), advertised as forming "the most practicable route from the coal fields and valuable deposits of iron from Alabama, to the harbor of Pensacola."[88]

The election of 1874 determined the fate of the Republican Party in Alabama. George Houston, poetically represented in Democratic literature and in Fleming's account as "The Bald Eagle of the Mountains," and as the defender of "White Supremacy," was elected by a large majority.[89] Neither the campaign literature nor Fleming referred to his close cooperation and participation in the Sloss and L. & N. enterprises. Almost too innocently, Fleming states that: "The campaign fund was the largest in the history of the State; every man who was able,

[81] Commercial and Financial Chronicle, Vol. XIX, No. 487, p. 423; Armes, op. cit., p. 252.

[82] Fleming, op. cit., pp. 583 ff.

[83] Henry W. Clews, Fifty Years in Wall Street, pp. 254 ff. New York: Irving Publishing Co., 1908.

[84] Ibid., p. 302.

[85] Ibid., p. 254.

[86] Ibid.

[87] Ibid.

[88] Armes, op. cit., p. 180; Kelley, The Old South and the New, passim; Poor's Manual, 1870–1871, p. 408.

[89] Fleming, op. cit., p. 793.

and many who were not, contributed; assistance also came from Northern Democrats, and Northern Capitalists who had investments in the South or *who owned part of the legal* bonds of the State."[90] As the "legality" of the bonds had not been determined at the time when these gentlemen made their contributions, the discrimination seems doubtful. Obviously the "Northern capitalists" who contributed to the Democratic fund did so *in the hope that with Democratic victory the bonds they owned would be declared legal by the new government.*[91] Nordhoff, a witness whose verdict was uncompromisingly against the Republican régime, said that "where conspicuous financial jobbery took place (in railroad legislation) Democrats have, oftener than not, been parties in interest."[92] Let us not forget what has already been noted; that as a specific effect of the Panic of 1873, it was the misfortune of the Republicans to enter the election of 1874 a year after the house of Jay Cooke had drawn Henry Clews with it to failure.[93]

There is a final incident to this industrial epic that may or may not have had a connection with the end of Reconstruction in Alabama in 1874, and in other states soon thereafter. On December 21, 1874, at Macon, Georgia, was formed what has been described as the "most efficient railroad pool in the United States, largely owing to the genius of Albert Fink as manager."[94]

Sharp competition first appeared after prostration by the Civil War, when it was soon discovered that there were more roads than available traffic. Agreements to restore and maintain charges alternated for a time with the most destructive rate wars. . . . Bankruptcy and ruin in railroad affairs were widespread. Permanent success was finally wrought out of such chaos by the first General Commissioner, who perfected an agreement in 1875 which proved lasting.[95]

The pool rejoiced in the innocent name of "The Southern Railroad and Steamship Company." It allayed competition, and facilitated the growth of several great systems where the highly individualistic small lines had flourished theretofore.[96] Coincident with the formation of this pool, it is interesting to note certain changes in the directorates of many of the Southern lines as reported for 1875–1876, and contrasted with the same lists for 1868–1869.[97] J. Pierpont Morgan, in 1875–1876, appears as a Director for several of the Alabama and Georgia lines, including the Mobile and Montgomery, an L. & N. affiliate.[98] Josiah Morris appears as a member of the directorate of the Mobile and Montgomery, the Western Railroad of Alabama (a Central of Georgia affiliate), and the South and North (L. & N. affiliate).[99] H. B. Plant, founder of the Plant system, appears as Director of the Western Railroad of Alabama.[100]

The election of Governor Houston in 1874 provided an opportunity for the settlement of the "debt" of Alabama, as pledged by the winning party. The debt

90 *Ibid.*, p. 792. Italics the author's.

91 Italics the author's.

92 Nordhoff, *The Cotton States in 1875*, p. 89.

93 Clews, *op. cit.*, passim.

94 William Z. Ripley, *Railroads: Finance and Organization*, p. 584. New York: Longmans, Green & Co., 1915. Fink, it will be remembered, was the guiding hand in the early L. & N. penetration of Alabama, and in that formulating the merger between the South and North and the L. & N. that defeated the designs of the Russell Sage, Republican, Alabama and Chattanooga.

95 *Ibid.*

96 Ripley, *op. cit.*, p. 585.

97 See *Poor's Railroad Manuals* for given years, passim.

98 *Poor's Railroad Manual*, 1876, p. 476.

99 *Ibid.*, pp. 476, 484, 671.

100 *Ibid.*, p. 484.

settlement is supposed to have been framed by a State Senator, Rufus W. Cobb, "and others."[101] Cobb, according to a biographical sketch, "devised the plan of readjustment for the state debt which Governor Houston submitted to the legislature after elaboration. He was the friend and admirer of Governor Houston during his administration."[102] Cobb was also President of the Central Iron and Coal Works at Helena, which was subsidized by the L. & N.[103] In addition, he was a local attorney for the L. & N.[104]

Governor Houston began his administration with the expressed desire of settling the "debt." It should be kept in mind here that "debts" are either paid, or repudiated; and those who, following Fleming, state that the "Reconstruction Debt" in Alabama amounted to from $25,000,000 to $30,000,000, need to ask themselves how a "debt" of this size, existing at the accession of Houston in 1874, could become a "debt" of less than $10,000,000 through his adjustments without actual repudiation. Certainly the Alabama "debt" was adjusted; but there was no repudiation. It will appear in the following paragraphs that the Alabama "debt" of $25,000,000 to $30,000,000 was not, at any time, an actual "debt," but always a potential one; and that if it had been, or become, an "actual debt," the State would have owned all of the railroads endorsed by it as compensation for the "debt" assumed. The long-heralded triumph of Governor Houston's "debt settlement" actually will be seen to have consisted in relieving the State of its "potential debt," and the railroads of the

threat of State foreclosure on mortgages held by it, on grounds highly advantageous to the railroads; or, at least, to those railroad systems with which the leadership of the Alabama Democracy was on a fairly intimate basis.

As his "debt commissioners" Governor Houston appointed Levi W. Lawler, T. B. Bethea, and himself as *ex-officio* chairman. T. B. Bethea does not appear as a director or stockholder in any published records of these facts.[105] Levi W. Lawler was reported in 1868[106] and 1870 as a director of the Selma, Rome, and Dalton,[107] a competing road to the Alabama and Chattanooga; Peter Hamilton, listed with Rufus Cobb as one of the men responsible for the debt settlement in preliminary negotiations, is recorded as a Mobile and Ohio (an L. & N. subsidiary) director in 1868,[108] and in 1870–1871.[109] Houston was a director of the Nashville and Decatur (an L. & N. affiliate) in 1868[110] and 1870;[111] his law partner, Luke Pryor, whom he followed to Washington as United States Senator from Alabama, was a director of the South and North (an L. & N. subsidiary) in 1870[112] and in 1875.[113]

The Report of the Debt Commissioners prefaced an analysis of the nature of State obligations by saying that the "direct and contingent indebtedness of the State is $30,000,000."[114] For political purposes, these obligations had been

101 Owens, *History of Alabama and Dictionary of Alabama Biography*, III, p. 357.
102 *Ibid.*
103 *Ibid.*; Armes, *op. cit.*, pp. 17, 147.
104 Owens, *op. cit.*, III, p. 357.

105 In *Affairs of Southern Railroads*, or in successive *Poor's Manuals*.
106 *Ibid.*, p. 384.
107 *Ibid.*, 1871, p. 393.
108 *Poor's Manual, 1869*, p. 104.
109 *Ibid.*, 1871, p. 268.
110 *Ibid.*, 1869, p. 266.
111 *Ibid.*, 1871, p. 114.
112 *Affairs of Southern Roads*, p. 122.
113 *Ibid.*, 1875, p. 671.
114 *House Journal, 1875–1876*, p. 192.

talked about during the campaign as though they were a "direct" debt; and the historians have not distinguished between the two classes. As suggested above, the greater part of this "debt" was *"contingent";* that is to say, it would become a direct debt only in the event that the State foreclosed its mortgages upon the railroad property, leaving the State in debt, indeed, to bondholders, to the amount of the endorsements and loans, but at the same time possessed of the valuable railroad properties as compensation.

The Debt Commission divided the said "indebtedness" into four classes. Class I was defined as including:

... bonds issued or loaned to railroad companies (consisting) of bonds bearing five, six, and eight per cent interest; bonds issued for temporary loans; bonds hypothecated with and sold by the New York Guaranty and Indemnity Company, on account of a temporary loan; bonds hypothecated with and sold by agencies appointed by the United States District Court, in bankrupt cases; State obligations, bearing eight per cent interest; State Certificates, known as "Patton money"; Trust funds, and some small claims against the State.[115]

This class of indebtedness amounted to $11,677,470, including $1,050,000 of unpaid interest. The great portion of this debt had accumulated prior to Republican rule in 1868; when this party had taken over control in 1868, the State bonded debt was $6,848,400, with $2,-494,654.87 of additional state funds which had been dissipated, but still involved the state in interest payments.[116] Obligations in Class I which might be laid to

"Reconstruction extravagance" therefore accounted for approximately one million of the total.

Class I debts were "settled" by a refunding operation by which the state was granted a lower rate of interest and the cancellation of past due interest payments.[117]

Class II amounted to $1,156,000. They represented the liability of the State for railroad endorsements compromised under the law of 1873, in Governor Lewis' administration, when the railroads had exchanged $4,000-a-mile bonds for the prior bonds valued at $18,000-a-mile. By this means the State had, by 1874, reduced its liability by retiring $5,103,000 worth of endorsed bonds.[118]

Class II debts were "settled" by exchanging endorsement bonds for one-half of their face value; in other words, admitted the Commission, the "State accepted a clear loss of one-half." The roads so favored were the (James Sloss–George Houston–Luke Pryor) L. & N. affiliate, the South and North; the Grand Trunk; and the Savannah and Memphis.[119]

Class III debts are called by Fleming "the worst of all."[120] They totalled $2,-573,093. These obligations included $600,000 of claims rendered by the South and North,[121] of which Governor Houston's law partner, Luke Pryor, was a director,[122] and in which, as we have seen, the omni-present James W. Sloss had been from the first a prominent figure. Governor Houston himself had been a director of the affiliated L. & N. company, the Nashville and Decatur, in

115 *Ibid.,* p. 193.

116 *Poor's Railroad Manual, 1869–1870,* p. 470.

117 *House Journal, 1875–1876,* p. 194.
118 *Ibid.,* p. 195.
119 *Ibid.,* pp. 195–196.
120 *Op. cit.,* p. 581.
121 *House Journal, 1875–1876,* p. 196.
122 *Poor's Railroad Manual, 1875–1876,* p. 671.

1868[123] and in 1870.[124] The South and North claims were actually L. & N. claims, since the company was a subsidiary of the greater line.

Regarding these claims, the Debt Commission, of which, it will be remembered, Governor Houston was Chairman, stated:

It is not our province to make any suggestion in regard to the claim of the South and North. . . . They are not connected in any way with the bonded debt of the State, and do not come within the scope of our investigation and adjustment.[125]

But this $600,000 had been included in the "debt" as originally claimed by the Democrats, and as quoted by later historians. To disregard it was one of the simpler devices for "settlement" and "reduction" adopted by the Debt Commission.

The Commission dealt less kindly with $1,464,689 of obligations which involved the banking house of Henry Clews & Company. Clews, we have observed, was a banking associate of Jay Cooke,[126] and in Alabama had investments at Anniston in the Oxford Iron Works along with Samuel Noble, erstwhile trader-between-the-lines, and William D. "Pig-Iron" Kelley.[127] Clews' interests had been with the Alabama and Chattanooga, the Russell Sage, Republican sponsored road that was intent on invading the Alabama Mineral District from the direction of Chattanooga as the L. & N. was similarly bent on tapping this region from the North.

Mr. Clews' autobiography states simply, but eloquently, that the Debt Commission was motivated by "political manipulations" in disposing of his claims.[128] This was their solemn pronouncement regarding the Clews obligation:

The State is liable only for the amount of the debt which was due to Clews and Co., amounting to about three hundred and ten thousand dollars, with interest. This amount is all that we recommend to be arranged by the State; and as to which of the claimants it belongs we do not undertake to decide."[129]

It was in this manner that another million of the "debt" was settled.

Class IV "debts" amounted to $14,-641,000. They consisted of endorsed bonds on the basis of $16,000 a mile which had not been compromised under the $4,000-a-mile law. The total obligation, on inspection by the Commission, was scaled down to $11,597,000,[130] excluding $3,024,000 in loans due from the Alabama and Chattanooga and the Montgomery and Eufaula with unpaid interest.[131] The "scaled down" figure of $11,597,000 included $5,300,000 worth of endorsements at $16,000-a-mile for the Alabama and Chattanooga, $3,474,000 worth of unpaid interest, and a $2,000,000 loan from the State to the Alabama and Chattanooga.[132]

It has been pointed out above that Governor Lindsay, Democrat, had thrown the Alabama and Chattanooga into the hands of the State in 1871.[133] Extensive litigation had resulted, the bondholders, most of whom were English, claiming that the State had deliberately wrecked

123 Ibid., 1868-1869, p. 266.
124 Ibid., 1870-1871, p. 393.
125 House Journal, 1875–1876, pp. 196–197.
126 See p. 333, above.
127 See p. 334, above.
128 Fifty Years in Wall Street, p. 255.
129 House Journal, 1875–1876, pp. 197–199; Ibid., 1876–1877, pp. 252–254.
130 House Journal, 1875–1876, p. 199.
131 Ibid.
132 Ibid.
133 See page 330, above.

the road.[134] Considering the fact that Clanton, whom Lindsay appointed as one of the receivers, was also Executive Chairman of the State Democratic Committee, as well as a leading figure in the competing L. & N. affiliates, the complaint had at least plausibility. The Debt Commission compromised the claims of the English bondholders by (a) paying them $1,000,000, thus disposing of the alleged nine million dollars of indebtedness charged against the State in this connection,[135] and (b) transferring to the owners of the railroad's first mortgage bonds more than a half million acres of land, in the heart of the rich mineral region, and which later became the scene of extensive industrialization in Alabama.[136]

The remaining items of endorsement, involving the Montgomery and Eufaula, the East Alabama and Cincinnati, the Selma and Gulf, the Selma, Marion and Memphis, and the New Orleans and Selma, were in litigation at the time of the Committee Report. The Commission stated that the action of the Court would probably result in nullifying the purported liability of the State, and that the interests of the bondholders would best be served by "their acceptance of a transfer of the lien of the State created by statute, and giving to the State a full discharge from those pretended claims against it."[137] In other words, the "Debt" Commission itself denominated as "pretended claims" large amounts which it afterward proudly claimed to have "set-

tled," and which historians have accepted as the "Alabama Debt."

The final report of the Debt Commission stated that: "the volume of indebtedness of the State, including State obligations, will be reduced to about $9,500,000 *exclusive of trust funds*."[138] Since the Commission had begun its first report by stating that the debt amounted to more than $30,000,000, this immense reduction was hailed as a triumph of Democratic honesty over Republican extravagance. It has been so regarded by practically all historians. More interesting still, the myth of an immense debt of $30,000,000, crushing the people of Alabama for two generations, has persisted along with the paradoxical belief that the Democratic Party, immediately on its return to power, rescued the State from an immense load of debt. To all intents and purposes, the debt existed for purposes of Democratic propaganda in the election of 1874; it ceased to exist in 1875–1876 for the purpose of showing Democratic honesty; but it has always existed to show how great was the ruin wreaked upon the State by the Republican, Reconstruction government.

Fleming's conclusion to a discussion of the debt situation remains in evidence as *the* perfect document:

There was not an honest white person who lived in the State during Reconstruction, nor a man, woman or child, descended from such a person, who did not then suffer or does not still suffer from the direct results of the carpet-bag-financiering. Homes were sold or mortgaged; schools were closed, and children grew up in ignorance; the taxes for nearly twenty years were used to pay interest on the debt then piled up. Not until 1899 was there a one-mill school tax (until then the interest paid on the Reconstruction debt was

---

134 (No author), *The Hill Country of Alabama, U.S.A.; or, the land of rest*, pp. 95–96. London: Published for the English Committee of Bondholders, 1878.

135 *House Journal, 1875–1876*, p. 191.

136 *Ibid.*; See also *The Hill Country of Alabama,* pp. 95–96.

137 *House Journal, 1875–1876*, p. 202.

138 *Ibid.*, pp. 53, 255.

larger than the school fund),[139] and not until 1891 was the state able to care for the disabled Confederate soldiers.[140]

Knight states that one of the reasons for the backwardness of Alabama in education was the fact that "upon Alabama was heaped a debt of $18,000,000."[141] Cubberley states, similarly, that the Reconstruction government caused backwardness in the schools through "wasting of resources."[142]

These statements may be seen to be exaggerated and incorrect, especially when they lay blame for immense "debts" upon "Negro," "Republican" régimes in Alabama. There was no "Negro" government; no such debts were left after Reconstruction; and what debts were created resulted from the activities of various capitalists working through both Republican and Democratic Party channels. The debt settlement of 1876 left the residual obligations of the State Government, including both bonded debt and the various trust funds for which the State was responsible, at approximately $12,000,000. It has been shown, above, that these same obligations in 1868, when the Reconstruction government took control, amounted approximately to $9,500,000.[143]

What is true is that in the negotiations leading up to the refunding of the debt, the holders of various State obligations drove a hard bargain with the Debt Commission regarding future tax policy. The Constitutional Convention of 1875 was in session while the debt negotiations were being held, and the articles adopted on taxation and finance were dictated by the arrangement with the bondholders. Considering their financial affiliations, it can be readily imagined that Governor Houston and his fellow-committeemen were all too eager to comply. On October 16, 1875, the Convention was reported on the verge of complete repudiation;[144] a combination of Black Belt Conservatives, not in the "ring," with hill country "radicals," were all for making trouble for the "debt" commission and its mission. The Committee on Taxation of the Convention reported that they had advised with General L. W. Lawler and Colonel T. B. Bethea, two of the three debt commissioners. These men were sanguine that the "debt" could be "reduced" from $30,000,000 to $10,000,000 through their negotiations, and advised the Convention to limit State tax levies to a maximum impost of .0075 on the dollar. If this were done, the debt commissioners believed that

Capital, seeing that our debt is reduced and our taxing power limited, will seek investment in our cheap lands, and population, always following capital, will fill up our waste places. . . . Capital (will see) that our property will enhance in value.[145]

In a letter written by the debt commissioners to the bondholders, dated December 30, 1875, it is revealed that

[139] The Brookings Institute, in a recent study of the Alabama financial structure, pointed out that the reason Alabama had an archaic tax limit for schools was because of a strangle-hold upon state government by planters and industrialists, who had engrafted this limitation in the State Constitution of 1875. See *Taxation of the State Government of Alabama*, p. 47, Vol. 4, Pt. 3. Montgomery: Wilson Printing Co., 1932.

[140] *Op. cit.*, pp. 585-586.

[141] Edgar W. Knight, *Education in the United States*, p. 468.

[142] Ellwood P. Cubberley, *Public Education in the United States*, p. 435. Cambridge: The Riverside Press, Houghton Mifflin Co., 1924.

[143] See page 338, above.

[144] *Commercial and Financial Chronicle*, Vol. XXI, No. 534, September 18, 1875, p. 276.

[145] *Journal of the Constitutional Convention of the State of Alabama of 1875*, pp. 35-36. Montgomery: W. W. Screws, State Printer, 1875.

the latter had made various suggestions regarding ways in which the expenses of the State could be cut, so as to allow payment of interest due on State obligations. One method suggested was to cut the size of appropriations made to the schools.[146] A second was to save money by cutting down the expenses of feeding prisoners.[147] In fact, the two fundamental anti-social weaknesses in Alabama's state government to comparatively modern times, i.e., poor schools and the convict lease system, were specifically suggested by the bondholders as possible sources of needed revenue.[148]

During debate, in the Alabama House, on a proposed tax bill, the estimate of the Debt Commission was taken as a guide for the House Committee. The Debt Commission estimated a total income of $1,066,000 would derive from a seven and one-half mill levy. State expenses were estimated at

State Government	$400,000
Interest, Trust Fund	100,000
Appropriation, School	100,000
Interest, Univ. Fund	24,000
Interest, A. & M. Bonds	20,280
Interest, State Obligations	54,000
Total	$798,000

This would leave $241,720 to pay interest on the various debts.[149] The refunding arrangement operated so that on several classes of obligations the interest began

146 *Commercial and Financial Chronicle, January 29, 1876,* Vol. XXII, No. 553, p. 110.

147 *Ibid.*

148 Governor Houston and his successor, Governor Cobb, who, as suggested above, were closely associated with James W. Sloss, turned the convict system from a liability into a profitable source of revenue for the State. See pages 321 and 322, above.

149 *House Journal, 1876–1877,* pp. 254–256; *Commercial and Financial Chronicle,* February 12, 1876, Vol. XXII, No. 555.

five years from the date of settlement, while on others interest was set at a low figure for the first few years.[150] The only provisions made for the support of schools were (a) the "Interest on the Trust Fund"; this meant that the interest upon the fictitious literary fund which had been dissipated in the failure of the State bank twenty years before, would be appropriated by the Legislature yearly to the support of the schools; and, (b), a yearly appropriation of $100,000 from the State Treasury.[151] The Constitution imbedded in the organic law of the State a fixed state tax levy maximum. This, together with the graduation of interest payments to increase over a period of years, and the Constitutional prohibition of local taxation for schools, effectually estopped any major increases in appropriations for schools so long as the Constitution of 1875 remained in force.[152]

Conclusion

The story of Reconstruction, as viewed in the foregoing pages, admittedly needs elaboration; it concerns itself unduly neither with whites, nor with blacks; with the State Legislature, nor with the Senate; with carpetbaggers, nor with scalawags; nor even with the senators, congressmen, governors, legislators, and other factotums usually accorded major attention.

Our story has sought to identify great social and economic forces whose working in Alabama during Reconstruction gives to the period the quality of inevitable, inexorable pressure and response, action and reaction. These forces are none the less significant because they lack tangible form, and frequently defy exact statistical description.

150 *Ibid.*

151 *House Journal, 1875–1876,* p. 204.

152 See *Brookings Institution Report, op. cit.*

We have seen that the land — Mother Earth — attracted and repelled different social and economic classes of white migrants, and so moulded the shape of institutions, and the ecology of their distribution. We have seen, further, that man-made institutions could become the source of attitudes which reciprocally reinforced the strength of the institution. The geography of Alabama determined the boundaries of the plantation system of cotton culture, and, together with the source of the migrants, defined the structure of chattel slavery in the State. The institution of chattel slavery in turn required the development of an elaborate set of mental attitudes bulwarking its structure. Social and economic classes among white persons depended for their form upon the nature of the land and the nature of the institution of Negro slavery, as well as upon "natural" principles of economic stratification. Each of these diversifying factors affected the institutions maintained, and, consequently, the attitudes derivative from them.

The natural endowment of the State with resources for an industrial civilization attracted capital bent on exploiting this mineral wealth. Our perspective enables us to perceive that accumulations of capital, and the men who controlled them, were as unaffected by attitudinal prejudices as it is possible to be. Without sentiment, without emotion, those who sought profit from an exploitation of Alabama's natural resources turned other men's prejudices and attitudes to their own account, and did so with skill and a ruthless acumen. Meanwhile, there were men of sentiment who had a mixed vision of another kind of social structure — the Northern Humanitarians, the landless whites and the landless Negroes. Recon-

struction in Alabama, during its first stages, was affected by 19th Century Humanitarianism, as it was finally determined by 19th Century capital expansion and exploitation. A decadent and para-lyzed agrarian structure founded on chattel slavery, in combination with political and economic forces working on a nation-wide scale, witnessed the defeat of the Humanitarian ideal and the triumph of the capital investor. Since, politically, Humanitarianism, as it had power to affect the government of the South, died with Thaddeus Stevens in 1868, Reconstruction after that date may be signalized as a struggle between different financiers. The panic of 1873, and the collapse of one of the contestants as a result, paved the way for the general peace that came in the period from 1874 to 1876.

In this retrospect such institutions as the Louisville and Nashville Railroad, the Alabama and Chattanooga Railroad, the Union League (considered as an instrument of Northern capital), the banking houses of the Cookes, of Russell Sage, of the Morgans and the Drexels, loom more significantly in Alabama Restruction than do the time-honored figures of the history books. Such personalities as James W. Sloss, Josiah Morris, Albert Fink, Henry Clews, Jay Cooke, William Kelley, Luke Pryor, Russell Sage, and V. K. Stevenson, assume larger proportions than all of the governors and legislators of whom such full account has been taken in the past.

We may even be tempted to conclude that the Carpetbaggers, the Scalawag, "Nigger domination," and even the Ku Klux Klan, were not the principal heroes, or the villains, of the Reconstruction period in Alabama.

Vernon Lane Wharton:
THE NEGRO IN MISSISSIPPI POLITICS

Negro Officials in County and
Municipal Governments

BY a provision of the new constitution of the state, the terms of all local officials expired with the readmission of Mississippi to the Union. Appointments to local offices were then to be made by the Governor with the advice and consent of the senate. Thus there were no municipal or county elections in the state until the fall of 1871. The Governor, J. L. Alcorn, as an old and relatively conservative citizen of the state, made appointments that at least were up to the usual standard for such officials. In some cases, the entire county lists were made up of Democrats or old Whigs.[1] Alcorn's selections for the judiciary were made up almost entirely of leading members of the state bar.[2] Altogether, the total of his appointments included 247 Republicans, 217 Democrats, and seventy-two members of other opposition groups.[3] So far as possible, Alcorn avoided the appointment of Negroes.[4] It appears that no member of that race except Robert H. Wood of Natchez was made mayor of any town.[5] With the possible exception

of Coffeeville and Greenville, no town had a Negro majority on its board of aldermen.

Even after the election of 1871, a Negro majority in a municipal government seems to have been unknown.[6] The city of Jackson, with a powerful Republican machine that maintained its control for thirteen years after the overthrow of the party in the state, only once had more than one Negro on its city council of six members. The one exception followed the election of 1874, when two Negroes became aldermen.[7] In Natchez, where the Negroes held an enormous majority, they placed only three members on a council of seven.[8] Efforts of the Negro majority to gain control of the board in Vicksburg in 1874 lost the support of the white members of their party, and with it the election.[9]

The chief complaint against the participation of the freedmen in the government of the towns grew out of their appointment as policemen. The presence of such officials helped to bring on the

phy" that John R. Lynch served as mayor of Natchez seems to be an error.

[1] Fred M. Witty, "Reconstruction in Carroll and Montgomery Counties, *P.M.H.S.*, X, 120.

[2] Mississippi *Weekly Pilot*, October 1, 1870; Hinds County *Gazette*, October 5, November 2, 1870; J. S. McNeily, "War and Reconstruction in Mississippi," *P.M.H.S.C.S.*, II, 393.

[3] Hinds County *Gazette*, September 6, 1871.

[4] Jackson *Clarion-Ledger*, November 27, 1890.

[5] Hiram Revels' statement in his "Autobiogra-

[6] John R. Lynch, *The Facts of Reconstruction*, p. 92.

[7] Goodspeed Publishing Company, *Biographical and Historical Memoirs of Mississippi*, II, 174.

[8] Edward King, *The Great South*, p. 293; Natchez *Tri-Weekly Democrat and Courier*, August 13, 1873.

[9] J. W. Garner, *Reconstruction in Mississippi*, pp. 329–330.

Vernon Lane Wharton, *The Negro in Mississippi, 1865–1890* (University of North Carolina Studies in History and Political Science, Chapel Hill: University of North Carolina Press, 1947), pp. 167–180. Used by permission.

Meridian riot in 1871,[10] and furnished the central theme of the attack on the Republican government in Jackson.[11] The general attitude of the whites, as expressed by Ethelbert Barksdale, was that "negroes ought not to be put in a position to discharge constabulary functions which it is proper for white men to exercise." Law enforcement implied domination, and as Barksdale said, the white race was "not in the habit of being dominated by the colored race."[12]

In general the few towns which had Republican governments as late as 1874 overthrew them before the state government fell in the fall of 1875. The Democrats took Vicksburg in August, 1874, and Columbus in December. Yazoo City was captured in April, 1875, and Okolona in August. The methods generally used in this process, combining persuasion, intimidation, economic pressure, and violence, were similar to those used later in the state campaign. For towns which had Negro majorities, the legislature assured the continuation of Democratic control by excluding from the corporate limits large portions of the Negro residential sections.[13] The one important exception to the overthrow of Republican municipal governments in the years 1874 and 1875 was the city of Jackson, where a peculiar situation and a large number of white votes maintained that party in power until 1888.

Very little information is available as to the participation of the Negroes in the various county governments. More than

half of the counties held white majorities, and most of these naturally eliminated in the elections of 1871 the few Negro officials appointed by Alcorn in 1870. In the elections of 1873, the Democrats carried thirty-nine of the seventy-four counties, and in 1875 sixty-two of the seventy-four. Of course, in several of the predominantly white counties, black beats at times elected one or two supervisors or justices of the peace. Yalobusha, Scott, and Lawrence counties, as examples, generally had one Negro supervisor on the board of five.[14] Such Negroes were almost entirely without influence, and generally found it to their advantage to be "very quiet, good negroes," to use the description given of those in Lawrence.[15]

Even in the minority of the counties which had Negro and Republican majorities the freedmen seldom obtained many of the offices. By 1873, however, they became assertive enough to take control of a number of counties in which the white population was small. In Marshall County, for example, three of the five supervisors were Negroes who could barely read and write.[16] The three on the board in Yazoo County, the three in Warren, four of the five in Madison, and all five in Issaquena were described as "illiterate."[17] In these counties, there were also varying numbers of Negro justices of the peace, few of whom were

[10] Report on the Condition of Affairs in the Late Insurrectionary States, "Mississippi," I, 479.

[11] Jackson Clarion-Ledger, December 26, 1889.

[12] Senate Miscellaneous Documents, no. 166, 50th Congress, 1st session, p. 276.

[13] J. C. Brown, "Reconstruction in Yalobusha and Grenada Counties," P.M.H.S., XII, 217, 269; Lee Richardson and Thomas D. Godman, In and Around Vicksburg, p. 97.

[14] J. C. Brown, op. cit., XIII, 270; Forrest Cooper, "Reconstruction in Scott County," P.M.H.S., XIII, 164; Hattie Magee, "Reconstruction in Lawrence and Jeff Davis Counties," P.M.H.S., XI, 175.

[15] H. Magee, op. cit., XI, 175.

[16] J. W. Garner, op. cit., p. 309.

[17] Senate Reports, no. 527, 44th Congress, 1st session, pp. 1704, 876, 616; J. W. Garner, op. cit., p. 310. Illiteracy was fairly common among the officials of the hill counties before the war. E. C. Coleman, "Reconstruction in Attala County," P.M.H.S., X, 149–150.

capable of carrying out properly even the simple duties of their office. There were also a small number of Negro chancery and circuit clerks varying in ability from an "illiterate" in Yazoo to the highly cultured L. J. Winston, who remained as circuit clerk in Adams County, under white Democratic control, until his appointment as collector of the port of Vicksburg in 1897. According to John R. Lynch, "Out of seventy-two counties in the State at that time, electing on an average twenty-eight officers to a county, it is safe to assert that not over five out of one hundred of such officers were colored men."[18] This statement seems to be approximately correct.

The most important office in the counties, both in responsibilities and in financial returns, was that of sheriff. According to Lynch, not more than twelve Negroes in Mississippi ever held this office.[19] Available material supplies the names Blanche K. Bruce of Bolivar, J. J. Evans of De Soto, John Brown of Coahoma, Winslow of Washington, Sumner of Holmes, Merrimon Howard of Jefferson, Peter Crosby of Warren, William McCary and Robert H. Wood of Adams, W. H. Harney of Hinds, Scott of Issaquena, and Joe Spencer Watkins of Monroe. In regard to Sumner and Watkins, there is almost no information. Of Blanche K. Bruce, it is sufficient to say that his handling of the office of sheriff fully merited the confidence of the white planters who supplied his bond of $120,000. The offices of Evans and Winslow seem to have been managed very largely by the whites who supplied their bonds.[20] Charges of embezzlement

against Evans,[21] an ex-slave who was described as a good, sound Negro, seem to have been entirely unjustified.[22] Scott, judged by his testimony before the Boutwell Committee, was a man of intelligence and ability who, although he was elected by the votes of the Negroes, was completely under the control of white Democrats. Almost exactly the same description applies to Merrimon Howard of Jefferson, although he at times showed a bit more independence than Scott.[23] John Brown, run out of Coahoma County after a "race riot" during the campaign of 1875, six years later was declared to have embezzled a large sum for which his sureties were liable.[24] Peter Crosby, whose violent expulsion by white leaguers led to the Vicksburg riots of 1874, was a member of the infamous ring of that city. Yet, strangely enough, subsequent examination of his accounts disclosed them to be entirely in order.[25] Nordhoff's statement that he was illiterate is incorrect.[26] W. H. Harney of Hinds County was a Canadian Negro of some education and ability. He was popular with whites and blacks alike until the development of the bitter campaign of 1875. Charges that he was from twelve to twenty-one thousand dollars short in his accounts occupied the courts for five years. Newspaper reports of the settlement are confusing and contradictory.[27] William McCary and Robert Wood were intelligent members of fami-

---

18 John R. Lynch, *op. cit.*, p. 93.

19 *Ibid.*, p. 17.

20 Irby C. Nichols, "Reconstruction in De Soto County," *P.M.H.S.*, XI, 307; *Senate Reports*, no. 527, 44th Congress, 1st session, p. 1446.

21 J. W. Garner, *op. cit.*, p. 306.

22 I. C. Nichols, *op. cit.*, p. 307.

23 *Senate Miscellaneous Documents*, no. 45, 44th Congress, 2d session, pp. 156–157.

24 Jackson *Weekly Clarion*, July 21, 1881.

25 Charles Nordhoff, *The Cotton States*, p. 79.

26 *Senate Reports*, no. 527, 44th Congress, 1st session, "Documentary Evidence," p. 85.

27 Hinds County *Gazette*, December 29, February 24, 1875, April 5, 1876, July 31, 1878, July 14, 1880, August 3, 1881; Jackson *Weekly Clarion*, July 14, 1881.

lies who had been free and respected residents of Natchez for several generations.[28] Their conduct seems to have given general satisfaction.

In regard to the quality and activity of county governments between 1870 and 1875, a few generalizations may be drawn. As compared with the period before the war, this was one of greatly increased activity. Bridges, roads, and public buildings destroyed or allowed to go to pieces during the war had to be reconstructed. In addition, the greatly increased business of country stores, the rapid growth of small towns, and expanded social and political activities called for the building of new roads. Under the new system of public education, there were schools to be built and a great number of teachers to be employed. The admission of the freedmen to the courts more than doubled their business. Then too, there was a great burst of enthusiasm for the building of railroads. County after county and town after town made contributions for this purpose after overwhelmingly favorable votes by whites and blacks, and Democrats and Republicans alike. All of this implied an enormous increase in county expenditures, and a proportional increase in taxation. Furthermore, the burden of this increase fell directly on the owners of real estate. The large revenue from the head-tax on slaves was no longer available, and the Republican party, made up largely of propertyless Negroes and of business and professional men, quickly lightened the heavy levies that formerly had been made on artisans, professional men, and commercial enterprisers.

Interestingly enough, there seems to be no correlation at all between the rate of taxation and the political or racial character of the counties. In 1874, at the height of Negro-Republican control, the average rate for the thirty-nine Democratic counties was $12\frac{7}{13}$ mills. That for the thirty-four Republican counties was $13\frac{7}{17}$ — a difference of less than one mill. The county tax in the Democratic units ranged from 6.2 mills in Pontotoc to 20.3 in Chickasaw. In the Republican counties, the range was from 5.3 in De Soto to 23.2 in Colfax. Negro influence was probably greatest in Madison, Issaquena, Amite, Washington, Warren, Yazoo, Wilkinson, and Hinds. As compared with a state average of 13, the rates in these counties were, respectively, 11, 16, 11, $13\frac{1}{2}$, 14, 10, 19, and 11.4 mills.[29] Warrants in counties with heavy Negro populations were running at from forty to seventy-five cents on the dollar.[30] On the other hand, those in Lee County, where no Negro or Republican of any kind ever held office, fell to thirty cents.[31] The conclusion must be drawn that everywhere in the state a large part of the increase in expenditures was unavoidable. Then too, the wave of extravagance which was sweeping the nation did not fail to touch Mississippi. To a certain extent, the situation probably reflects the new feeling of self-importance and the new influence that had come to the poor whites.

The question of how much fraud existed in the various counties is difficult to answer. Charges, in general terms, were frequently made in the Democratic press. The leading Republican paper assembled the available evidence, and attempted to show that a great deal more

[28] Natchez *Daily Courier*, November 8, 1866; John R. Lynch, *Some Historical Errors of James Ford Rhodes*, pp. 17–18.

[29] Mississippi *Weekly Pilot*, January 1, 23, 1875; J. W. Garner, *op. cit.*, p. 313.

[30] Vicksburg *Times and Republican*, February 2, 1873.

[31] W. H. Braden, "Reconstruction in Lee County," *P.M.H.S.*, X, 136.

dishonesty had been uncovered in Democratic than in Republican counties.[32] With the exception of J. H. Jones, who charges graft in Wilkinson,[33] it is the general conclusion of the few students who have investigated individual counties that while there was some extravagance, there is no evidence of open fraud.[34] Their conclusions are hard to reconcile with the many charges which were prevalent at the time.

There can be little doubt that there was a rotten situation in Vicksburg, a city which seldom knew an honest government before the war, and has almost never had one since. City expenditures were enormous. Most of them went for improvement of streets and wharves, and other projects which were really necessary for a town that was rapidly becoming a city, but if half of the charges of extravagance and graft were true, the city was getting little for its money. In this exploitation, Democrats and Republicans shared alike. It is also true that the enormous grants to railroads met almost no opposition at the polls.[35] It is therefore difficult to say just how much of the extravagance and corruption was real, or how much of it should be charged to Negroes and white Republicans.

The Vicksburg ring also controlled the government of Warren County, and there can be little doubt, in spite of the curious fact that Sheriff Crosby's accounts were found to be in order, that several of the county officials, Negroes and whites, were engaged in extensive embezzlement

through such methods as the forgery of warrants.[36] Unfortunately, it must be recorded that the thrifty black and white taxpayers who joined the violent white "Modocs" in overthrowing the Republican city government in 1874, and the county government in the following year, saw control pass into the hands of the least desirable element of the whites. The result was that conditions in city and county became worse rather than better.[37]

In conclusion it may be stated that although Negroes formed a majority of the population in thirty counties in Mississippi, they almost never took advantage of their opportunity to place any large number of their race in local offices. Of those who did hold offices, the twelve sheriffs were moderately satisfactory; most of them were at least capable of exercising the functions of their office. No Negro in the state ever held any higher judicial office than that of justice of the peace, and those who held that office seem generally to have been incompetent. Among the small number of chancery and circuit clerks there was a wide range of ability; most of them were not suitable men for their positions. Negroes who gained election to the boards of supervisors of the various counties, even in those cases where they formed a majority, generally were dominated by white Republicans, either natives or Northerners. Although many of the Negro supervisors were ignorant and incompetent, little difference can be discovered in the administration of their

[32] Mississippi *Weekly Pilot*, October 23, 1875.

[33] J. H. Jones, "Reconstruction in Wilkinson County," *P. M.H.S.*, VIII, 164.

[34] F. M. Witty, *op cit.*, X, 119, 120, 122; E. C. Coleman, *op. cit.*, X, 150, 155, 156, 161; W. H. Braden, *op. cit.*, 136; R. Watkins, *op. cit.*, XII, 183, 208; H. Magee, *op. cit.*, XI, 181.

[35] C. Nordhoff, *op. cit.*, p. 76; Hinds County *Gazette*, July 31, 1872.

[36] J. W. Garner, *op. cit.*, p. 293; Mississippi *Weekly Pilot*, March 6, 1875.

[37] C. Nordhoff, *op. cit.*, pp. 76, 81–82; Hinds County *Gazette*, April 21, 1875; Mississippi *Weekly Pilot*, August 21, 1875; Vicksburg *Herald*, August 17, 1875; Hinds County *Gazette*, June 19, 1878, February 3, 1883.

counties and that of counties under Democratic control.

Negroes and State Government

The first legislature under the new constitution assembled in Jackson in January, 1870. Of the 107 men in the house of representatives, twenty-five were Democrats and eighty-two were Republicans. The number of Negro representatives, originally thirty-one, was immediately reduced to thirty by the death of C. A. Yancey of Panola County. Thus, in a state which held a large Negro majority, members of that race made up less than two-sevenths of the total membership of the house, and less than three-eighths of the Republican majority. Their representation in the senate was even smaller. In the total membership of thirty-three, and in a Republican group of twenty-eight, only five were Negroes.[38]

Of the thirty Negroes in the house, eight had served in the constitutional convention. A dozen or more of the group, either by education or unusual native ability, were entirely capable of meeting their obligations as legislators. Among these were H. P. Jacobs, Henry Mayson, J. F. Boulden, M. T. Newsome, Merrimon Howard, John R. Lynch, J. Aaron Moore, H. M. Foley, J. J. Spelman, and J. H. Piles. All of these men made distinguished records in fields other than politics. Almost as capable were Albert Johnson, Nathan McNeese, A. K. Davis, Doctor Stites, Emanuel Handy, Richard Griggs, and W. H. Foote. The other fourteen members were inclined to be self-effacing, and took little part in the formation of policy.

Of the five members of the senate, three, Charles Caldwell, Hiram Revels,

and T. W. Stringer, have already been discussed. Robert Gleed, of Columbus, was a man of fair education, good character, and some financial ability, although he had been a slave until the close of the war.[39] An excellent speaker, he was employed by the Democratic administration after the overthrow of the Republican régime to lecture to the Negroes of the state on educational and agricultural matters. The fifth senator, William Gray of Greenville, was a young Baptist preacher of some education and much natural cleverness. A leader in the demands for civil rights for Negroes, he was lacking in tact, and was probably at times guilty of double-dealing both in politics and in religious affairs.

The election of a new house of representatives in 1871, for the term of 1872 and 1873, brought a heavy reduction of the Republican majority. Of the 115 members, the Republicans claimed sixty-six. Actually, however, several of the white members of their group, calling themselves independents, generally voted with the Democrats and against the administration. Negro membership rose to thirty-eight, but R. R. Applewhite of Copiah was completely under Democratic control, and later announced himself a member of that party. The Negroes now had a theoretical control of the Republican caucus in the lower house, but actually any attempt to press their advantage was generally blocked by the desertion of a number of their white colleagues. It was only after Alcorn urged it as a political necessity that John R. Lynch received enough white Republican votes to gain the speakership.

---

[38] J. S. McNeily, "War and Reconstruction in Mississippi," *P.M.H.S.C.S.*, II, 381; John R. Lynch, *The Facts of Reconstruction*, pp. 44–45.

[39] J. W. Garner Papers, Mississippi State Archives, Alexander Warner to J. W. Garner, May 4, 1900; J. W. Gardner, *op. cit.*, p. 295; *Senate Reports*, no. 527, 44th Congress, 1st session, p. 795.

It may therefore be said that during the first four years of Republican control the dominant group in both houses of the legislature was a combination of native and Northern white Republicans, who were influenced by the desires of their Negro constituents, but were also attentive to the large white element in their party, an element whose numbers they earnestly desired to increase. Their leader until late in 1871 was Governor Alcorn, an old Whig with Hamiltonian sentiments and a dream of bringing into the Republican party of the state men in the Democratic and Conservative groups who shared his beliefs. When Alcorn resigned in November, 1871, to take his place in the United States Senate, he was succeeded by R. C. Powers, a man of the same sentiments.[40] Both of these men wished to carry out a program which they considered to be for the best interests of whites and blacks alike. Both of them, like many of the White Republicans in the legislature, avoided social contacts with the Negroes as much as possible, and were absolutely opposed to any real control of their party by the Negroes.

In this situation, the Negro minority in the legislature generally followed the lead of the white Republicans, with whom, in matters of routine legislation, they were usually naturally in accord. In such routine business, the more able Negroes, including Stringer, Boulden, Jacobs, Spelman, and Lynch, were about as prominent as any of the white leaders. In fact, when the proportion of their numbers is kept in mind, a survey of the *Journals* reveals little difference between the whites and Negroes in attendance, in service on committees, or in activity on the floor. Negro members almost never suggested legislation to obtain special privileges for their race. The more able Negroes either recognized the weakness of their position or had no desire to gain undue advantage. The few who would have gone further received no encouragement or support.

In his inaugural address, in January, 1870, Governor Alcorn outlined clearly the two basic problems faced by the Republicans. "The obligations resting on us under the new order of things," he said, "extend very greatly the breadth of duty of the State Government. The 'patriarchal' groupings of our society in the days of slavery, confined the work of our political organizations, to a very great extent, to the heads of what we called 'families.'" Under the new régime, every individual had become a distinct entity. In addition to the great increase in the number of individuals concerned, a large increase in the *amount* of government was contemplated. The costs of the new administration must be much greater than those of the old. He would therefore urge the legislature to take advantage of every opportunity for economy. In regard to the state's new citizens, he said: "In the face of memories that might have separated them from me as the wronged from the wronger, they have offered me their confidence. . . . In response to that touching reliance, the most profound anxiety with which I enter my office . . . is that of making the colored man the equal, before the law, of any other man. . . ."[41] Thus, in the beginning, Alcorn presented the problems that doomed the Republican régime. There were many whites who were alienated by the extension of the powers of the state, and even more by the increase in costs and taxes. A

---

40 J. W. Garner, *op. cit.*, p. 281; Dunbar Rowland, *History of Mississippi*, II, 176; J. S. McNeily, *op. cit.*, II, 426.

41 Mississippi *House Journal*, 1870, pp. 56–57.

larger group, including, to a certain extent, Alcorn himself, absolutely refused to accept the implications of Negro equality before the law. Such revolutions, unless maintained by overwhelming force, cannot be accomplished in a decade.

With a treasury balance of about fifty dollars in cash and five hundred dollars in negotiable paper, the Republicans entered upon the program that was to reconstruct the state. During the next four years, they set up, organized, and maintained at state expense a bi-racial system of common school education which, although it did not approach the national average in facilities or expense, was an amazing advance beyond anything the state had known before. They gave state support to normal schools at Holly Springs and Tougaloo, and established Alcorn as a Negro counterpart to the state university. They completely reorganized, coordinated, and centralized the state judiciary, and gave to it a new code of laws. Old public buildings were renovated and enlarged and new ones were constructed. State hospitals were set up and supported at Natchez and Vicksburg, and the facilities of the state asylums for the blind, deaf and dumb, and insane were greatly expanded. All racial discrimination was eliminated from the laws of the state. Finally, after much disagreement, the legislature granted to the Negroes in 1873 a civil rights bill, which in theory guaranteed to them equal access to all places of public entertainment.

Although much of this legislation was expensive, and almost all of it was controversial, a partial acceptance of the program and a loss of faith in the Democratic party produced a sweeping victory in 1872, and the election of Republicans to five of the six congressional seats. By the summer of 1873, the Republican party had reached the height of its power in the state. In this very strength, however, there was a great weakness. The breakdown of Democratic opposition, in the state as in the nation, opened the way for a struggle among the discordant elements in the dominant party. Between 1867 and 1872, it had appeared that this struggle, when it came, would involve a choice by the Negroes between Northern and native whites as their leaders.[42] In spite of efforts of the Democrats to aggravate differences on this basis, it had greatly declined in importance by 1873. The great line of division had come to be the question of the extent to which Negroes were to be allowed to hold offices and to dominate the councils of the party.

This became apparent in the state and county conventions in the summer of 1873. The Negroes, after six years of domination of the party by whites, now declared that they must have a larger share of the offices. Although, in general, their demands were not yet proportional to their party membership, the Negroes overestimated their ability to supply suitable candidates. This became evident when, after Bruce's refusal to accept the lieutenant-governorship, that office went to the weak A. K. Davis. Matters became worse when the Vicksburg ring, threatening violence and secession, secured the post of superintendent of education for Cardozo. This left James Hill, candidate for the office of secretary of state, as the only really acceptable candidate offered by the Negroes for the three state positions which they demanded. Similar weaknesses were to be found in many of

42 Hinds County *Gazette*, November 1, 1867, July 5, August 9, 30, 1871.

the men whom they chose for places in the legislature and in the county governments. The most important point at issue, however, was the fact that it was now clear that actual domination of the party by the mass of its Negro membership would probably come in the near future. By thousands of white members of the party, and by a majority of its white leaders, such a development could not be accepted.

J. L. Alcorn, already repudiated by the Negroes, undertook to lead the opposition, and announced his candidacy for the governorship in opposition to Adelbert Ames. With him went most of the Republican leaders who were native whites, and a number of those from the North. To this group, calling itself the "Republican Party of Mississippi," the Democrat-Conservative organization immediately threw its support.[43]

In an election in which the color line was rather sharply drawn, Ames defeated Alcorn by a vote of 69,870 to 50,490. Seventy-seven of the 115 members of the lower house were Republicans of either the Alcorn or the Ames faction. Fifty-five were Negroes, but one or two of these were Democrats. In a senate of thirty-seven members, twenty-five were Republicans, including nine Negroes. All of the seven state officers were regular Ames Republicans, and three of them, the lieutenant-governor, the secretary of state, and the superintendent of education, were Negroes. Furthermore, a Negro from Warren County, I. D. Shadd, soon became the none-too-competent speaker of the house.

In his inaugural address, Governor Ames made a good impression. After pledging himself to work for economy and reform, he turned to the race problem, analyzed the causes of conflict, and called for tolerance and a mutual recognition of rights and interests.[44] Thus, as Alcorn had done four years before, Ames recognized the two great problems which neither of them could solve. The elevation of the Negro involved a rapid expansion of state services which were inconsistent with the old ideas of economy. The readjustment of the relationship between the races was a matter beyond the power of the governor or the legislature.

The heavy increase in the number of Negroes in the government of the state did not greatly decrease its efficiency or change its character. The secretary of state was both competent and honest, and the superintendent of education at least was competent. The Negro legislators, as a group, were fairly capable of handling their duties, and probably represented their race more worthily than did the Negroes in any other Southern legislature. Visiting the state in 1874, Edward King wrote:

. . . [Negroes] lounge everywhere, and there are large numbers of smartly dressed mulattoes, or sometimes full blacks, who flit here and there with the conscious air which distinguishes the freedman. I wish here to avow, however, that those of the negroes in office, with whom I came in contact in Mississippi, impressed me much more powerfully as worthy, intelligent, and likely to progress, than many whom I saw elsewhere in the South. There are some who are exceedingly capable, and none of those immediately attached to the government at Jackson are incapable. In the Legislature there are now and then negroes who are ignorant; but of late both branches have been freer of this curse than have those of Louisiana or South Carolina.

---

[43] *Appleton's Cyclopedia,* 1873, p. 514.

[44] Mississippi *Senate Journal,* 1874, pp. 24–25.

A visit to the Capitol showed me that the negroes, who form considerably more than half the population of Mississippi, had certainly secured a fair share of the offices. Colored men act as officials or assistants in the offices of the Auditor, the Secretary of State, the Public Library, the Commissioner of Emigration [sic], and the Superintendent of Public Instruction. The Secretary of State [James Hill], who has some negro blood in his veins, is the natural son of a well-known Mississippian of the old régime, formerly engaged in the politics of his State; and the Speaker of the House of Representatives at the last session was a black man. The blacks who went and came from the Governor's office seemed very intelligent, and some of them entered into general conversation in an interesting manner.[45]

In spite of Ames' evidently sincere interest in economy, he and his legislature found it very difficult to make any substantial reduction in the expenses of the state government. Under the Republican administration, expenses had grown to what the Democrats declared were fantastic proportions. As a matter of fact, when the abnormal years of the war are omitted, the figures of the state auditors do give the impression that the Republican administrations were extravagant:

Year	Democratic Administrations
1856 through 1860 — average	$ 767,438.78
1865	1,410,250.13
1866	1,860,809.89
1867	625,817.80
1868	525,678.80
1869	463,219.71
1876	518,709.03
1877	697,018.86
1878	707,022.46
1879	553,326.81
1880	803,191.31

45 Edward King, *The Great South*, pp. 314–315.

Year	Republican Administrations
1870	$1,061,249.90
1871	1,729,046.34
1872	1,596,828.64
1873	1,450,632.80
1874	1,319,281.60
1875	1,430,192.83

Thus the average yearly cost of the state government under the six years of Republican control was $1,431,205.35, or almost twice the normal expenditure of the years immediately preceding the war. Even more spectacular, however, had been the increase in taxation of real estate. For many years, real property had been practically exempt from taxation in Mississippi. In 1869, the last year of Democratic control, the rate on this class of property was only one mill, or a tax of only twenty dollars a year on a plantation assessed by its owner at twenty thousand dollars and worth perhaps fifty thousand. The great sources of revenue were a tax of a dollar a bale on cotton, and privilege and license taxes which seem to have been inordinately high. The Republican régime reversed this system; after abolishing the tax on cotton and almost entirely eliminating the privilege taxes, the Republicans placed almost the entire burden of the support of the state on real and personal property. The result was a rate that rose from five mills in 1871 to fourteen in 1874. However pleasing such a system might be to the advocate of the single tax, there can be no doubt that it brought wrath to the landowners in a period of agricultural depression.

So strong had the protest of the landowners become by the spring of 1875 that the legislature could no longer afford to overlook it. Governor Ames insisted that changes were necessary, and the representatives undertook the problem.

The reductions for which they provided, like those made later by the Democrats, were more apparent than real. For a centralized government in a state of more than a million people, it was a simple fact that a cost of $1,400,000 per year was not extravagant. To meet the situation, the legislature put back on the counties the cost of jury, witness, and inquest fees that had been assumed by the state. Thus, at one blow, an item of two hundred thousand dollars a year was chopped from the cost of the government of the state, but it was added to that of the counties. In addition; the legislature presented to the people a constitutional amendment to provide for a great reduction in the number of the circuit judges. It also reduced printing costs by cutting down the number of the legislative journals, and by eliminating the publication of departmental reports. Then, against the opposition of about half of the Negro members, it reduced the salaries of the governor and other state officials, and provided for biennial rather than annual sessions of the legislature. Appropriations to the state universities were reduced, and scholarships were abolished. Another amendment to the constitution provided for the distribution of income from state lands, fines, and liquor licenses rather than their incorporation in the permanent school endowment fund. The ratification of this amendment was to allow a heavy reduction in the state school tax. Finally, turning to the system of taxation, the legislature reduced the *ad valorem* levy to nine and one-fourth mills, placed a tax on railroads, and made a partial return to the use of privilege taxes.[46] Ironically enough, the effect of most of these reforms could not become apparent until the following year, at which time

their benefits were easily claimed by the triumphant Democrats. Their adoption went almost unnoticed in the midst of the tumultuous movement toward the revolution of 1875.

Unlike the Republican administrations in most of the other Southern states, those in Mississippi financed their enterprises almost entirely through taxation. When the party assumed control in January, 1871, the state had an empty treasury and a debt of $1,178,175.33.[47] When the Democrats returned to power in January, 1876, they found $524,388.68 in the treasury and a debt of $3,341,162.89.[48] With the deduction in each case of permanent funds which the state owed to itself, and consideration of the treasury balance, the payable debt in 1876, as in 1871, was approximately half a million dollars, a negligible amount.

Furthermore, the Republican state régime left a remarkable record of honesty. The conclusion of J. W. Garner seems to be approximately correct:

So far as the conduct of state officials who were entrusted with the custody of public funds is concerned, it may be said that there were no great embezzlements or other cases of misappropriation during the period of Republican rule. . . . The treasurer of the Natchez hospital seems to have been the only defaulting state official during the administration of Governor Ames. He was a carpetbagger, and the amount of the shortage was $7,251.81. The colored state librarian during Alcorn's administration was charged with stealing books from the library. The only large case of embezzlement during the postbellum period was that of the Democratic treasurer in 1866. The amount of the shortage was $61,962.[49]

[46] Mississippi *Session Laws*, 1875.

[47] Mississippi *Senate Journal*, 1872, *Appendix*, p. 125.

[48] Mississippi Auditor of Public Accounts, *Report*, 1876.

[49] J. W. Garner, *op. cit.*, pp. 322–323.

It may be added that the next embezzlement of any importance was that of the Democratic "redemption" treasurer who was elected in 1875. His shortage was $315,612.19.[50]

Altogether, as governments go, that supplied by the Negro and white Republicans in Mississippi between 1870 and 1876 was not a bad government. Never, in state, counties, or towns, did the Negroes hold office in proportion to their numbers, although their demands in this direction were undeniably increasing. The Negroes who held county offices were often ignorant, but under the control of white Democrats or Republicans they supplied a form of government which differed little from that in counties where they held no offices. The three who represented the state in the national Congress were above reproach. Those in

[50] Hinds County *Gazette*, March 22, 1890; J. Dunbar Rowland, *History of Mississippi*, II, 242–245; J. D. Rowland, *Encyclopedia of Mississippi History*, II, 743–744.

the legislature sought no special advantages for their race, and in one of their very first acts they petitioned Congress to remove all political disabilities from the whites. With their white Republican colleagues, they gave to the state a government of greatly expanded functions at a cost that was low in comparison with that of almost any other state. The legislature of 1875 reduced that cost to some extent, and opened the way for further reductions by the passage of constitutional amendments. It also removed some of the apparent injustices in the system of taxation. But one situation it did not alter. The Republican party had come to be branded as a party of Negroes, and it was apparent that the Negroes were more and more determined to assert their right to control that party. It is also true that many of the Negroes, probably a majority, favored a further expansion of the functions of the state, entirely at the expense, according to the whites, of white tax-payers. The way was open for the formation of a "white-line" party.

W. E. Burghardt Du Bois:

THE BLACK PROLETARIAT IN SOUTH CAROLINA

A GREAT political scientist in one of the oldest and largest of American universities wrote and taught thousands of youths and readers that "There is no question, now, that Congress did a monstrous thing, and committed a great

political error, if not a sin, in the creation of this new electorate. It was a great wrong to civilization to put the white race of the South under the domination of the Negro race. The claim that there is nothing in the color of the skin from the

From *Black Reconstruction*, by W. E. B. Du Bois, copyright 1935, by Harcourt, Brace and Company. Used by permission.

point of view of political ethics is a great sophism. A black skin means membership in a race of men which has never of itself succeeded in subjecting passion to reason; has never, therefore, created any civilization of any kind."[1]

Here is the crux of all national discussion and study of Reconstruction. The problem is incontinently put beyond investigation and historic proof by the dictum of Judge Taney, Andrew Johnson, John Burgess and their confreres, that Negroes are not men and cannot be regarded and treated as such.

The student who would test this dictum by facts is faced by this set barrier. The whole history of Reconstruction has with few exceptions been written by passionate believers in the inferiority of the Negro. The whole body of facts concerning what the Negro actually said and did, how he worked, what he wanted, for whom he voted, is masked in such a cloud of charges, exaggeration and biased testimony, that most students have given up all attempt at new material or new evaluation of the old, and simply repeated perfunctorily all the current legends of black buffoons in legislature, golden spittoons for fieldhands, bribery and extravagance on an unheard-of scale, and the collapse of civilization until an outraged nation rose in wrath and ended the ridiculous travesty.

And yet there are certain quite well-known facts that are irreconcilable with this theory of history. Civilization did not collapse in the South in 1868–1876. The charge of industrial anarchy is faced by the fact that the cotton crop had recovered by 1870, five years after the war, and by 1876 the agricultural and even commercial and industrial rebirth of the South was in sight. The public debt was

[1] John W. Burgess, *Reconstruction and the Constitution*, p. 133.

large; but measured in depreciated currency and estimated with regard to war losses, and the enlarged functions of a new society, it was not excessive. The legislation of this period was not bad, as is proven by the fact that it was retained for long periods after 1876, and much of it still stands.

One must admit that generalizations of this sort are liable to wide error, but surely they can justifiably be balanced against the extreme charges of a history written for purposes of propaganda. And above all, no history is accurate and no "political science" scientific that starts with the gratuitous assumption that the Negro race has been proven incapable of modern civilization. Such a dogma is simply the modern and American residue of a universal belief that most men are sub-normal and that civilization is the gift of the Chosen Few.

Since the beginning of time, most thinkers have believed that the vast majority of human beings are incorrigibly stupid and evil. The proportion of thinkers who believed this has naturally changed with historical evolution. In earliest times all men but the Chosen Few were impossible. Before the middle class of France revolted, only the Aristocracy of birth and knowledge could know and do. After the American experiment a considerable number of thinkers conceived that possibly most men had capabilities, except, of course, Negroes. Possibly never in human history before or since have so many men believed in the manhood of so many men as after the Battle of Port Hudson, when Negroes fought for Freedom.

All men know that by sheer weight of physical force, the mass of men must in the last resort become the arbiters of human action. But reason, skill, wealth, machines and power may for long periods enable the few to control the many. But to what end? The current theory of democracy is that dictatorship is a stopgap pending the work of universal education, equitable income, and strong character. But always the temptation is to use the stopgap for narrower ends, because intelligence, thrift and goodness seem so impossibly distant for most men. We rule by junta; we turn Fascist, because we do not believe in men; yet the basis of fact in this disbelief is incredibly narrow. We know perfectly well that most human beings have never had a decent human chance to be full men. Most of us may be convinced that even with opportunity the number of utter human failures would be vast; and yet remember that this assumption kept the ancestors of present white America long in slavery and degradation.

It is then one's moral duty to see that every human being, to the extent of his capacity, escapes ignorance, poverty and crime. With this high ideal held unswervingly in view, monarchy, oligarchy, dictatorships may rule; but the end will be the rule of All, if mayhap All or Most qualify. The only unforgivable sin is dictatorship for the benefit of Fools, Voluptuaries, gilded Satraps, Prostitutes and Idiots. The rule of the famished, unlettered, stinking mob is better than this and the only inevitable, logical and justifiable return. To escape from ultimate democracy is as impossible as it is for ignorant poverty and crime to rule forever.

The opportunity to study a great human experiment was present in Reconstruction, and its careful scientific investigation would have thrown a world of light on human development and democratic government. The material today, however, is unfortunately difficult to find. Little effort has been made to preserve the records of Negro effort and speeches, actions, work and wages, homes and families. Nearly all this has gone down beneath a mass of ridicule and caricature, deliberate omission and misstatement. No institution of learning has made any effort to explore or probe Reconstruction from the point of view of the laborer and most men have written to explain and excuse the former slaveholder, the planter, the landholder, and the capitalist. The loss today is irreparable, and this present study limps and gropes in darkness, lacking most essentials to a complete picture; and yet the writer is convinced that this is the story of a normal working class movement, successful to an unusual degree, despite all disappointment and failure.

South Carolina has always been pointed to as the typical Reconstruction state. It had, in 1860, 412,320 Negroes and 291,300 whites. Even at the beginning of the nineteenth century, the 200,000 whites were matched by 150,000 Negroes, and the influx from the Border and the direct African slave trade brought a mass of black slaves to support the new Cotton Kingdom. There had always been small numbers of free Negroes, a little over 3,000 at the beginning of the century, and nearly 10,000 in 1860.

It was estimated by the census that land values declined 60% between 1860–1867, and that all farm property, between 1860–1870, decreased from $169,738,630 to $47,628,175. In May, 1865, a meeting was held in Charleston, and a committee was sent to talk with President Johnson. He asked them to submit a list of names from which he might select a Provisional Governor, and he finally selected Benjamin F. Perry. This was, on the whole, an unfortunate selection. Perry was a devoted follower of Johnson, and believed that Johnson had the power and backing to put his policies through. He immediately succeeded in having all Negro troops withdrawn, and he was certain that the North was with him and Johnson in standing for a purely white man's government.

The Johnson convention met and took some advance steps. By a small majority, they did away with property qualifications for members of the legislature, but refused to count Negroes as basis of apportionment. This was a blow at the former slaveholders, and a step toward democracy so far as the whites were concerned, but it was coupled with absolute refusal to recognize the Negroes. Perry insisted on letting property retain its right of representation in the legislature, despite the opposition of President Johnson.

The convention wanted to abolish slavery only on condition that Negroes be confined to manual labor, and that slave owners be compensated. They were given to understand, however, that Johnson would not accept this, and they finally declared that since the slaves had been emancipated by the United States, slavery should not be reestablished. In the elections for this convention, there was little interest. Only about one-third of the normal vote was cast on the coast, and inland, there were, in many cases, no elections at all.

In the election which followed again only 19,000 votes were cast. Ex-Governor Orr received a small majority, and would have been beaten by Wade Hampton, if Hampton had not refused the use of his name. Orr was a man of striking personality, and had once been Speaker of the United States House of Representatives.

The legislature which met after this election passed one of the most vicious of the Black Codes. It provided for corporal punishment, vagrancy and apprentice-ship laws, openly made the Negro an inferior caste, and provided special laws for his governing.

Neither humanity nor expediency demanded such sharp distinctions between the races in imposing punishments. The restriction of Negro testimony to cases in which the race was involved was not common sense. The free admission of such testimony in all cases would not have involved the surrender of power by the whites since they were to be the judges and jury. The occupational restrictions, instead of tending to restore order, created the impression that the dominant race desired to exclude the blacks from useful employment. It was impractical for a poverty-stricken commonwealth to have projected such elaborate schemes of judicial and military reorganization.[2]

There was increased difficulty in the economic situation. The war had ended late in the spring of 1865, so that the crops of that year were short, and there were crop failures for the next two years. All this complicated matters. In addition to this, the splendid start which the Negroes had on the lands of Port Royal, and on the Sea Islands, was interrupted. Johnson's proclamation and orders of 1865 provided for the early restoration of all property except property in slaves and such of the Port Royal lands as had been sold for taxes. The landlords hurried to get their pardons and to take back their lands. The Negroes resisted sometimes with physical force. When some of the landlords visited Edisto Island, the Negroes told them:

You had better go back to Charleston, and go to work there, and if you can do nothing else, you can pick oysters and earn your living.

2 Simkins and Woody, *South Carolina During Reconstruction*, pp. 51–52.

But these white men were not used to earning their own living. They were used to having Negroes do that for them, and now they had the Federal Government back of their claims. General Howard came down to facilitate the transfer and explain the condition to the Negroes. Still the black folk were dissatisfied. They drew up a petition to President Johnson, asking for at least an acre and a half of land. The planters became overbearing and the Negroes angry. Saxton, who had placed them on the land, was dismissed, and Howard deprived of his power. So that finally, by Federal force, Negroes were compelled to leave most of the lands and to make contracts as common laborers. The third Freedmen's Bureau Bill gave this the force of law. Thousands of Negroes migrated to Florida during 1866–1867, because of the land difficulties, the labor contracts, and the crop failures. Two thousand five hundred migrated to Liberia.

Landholders used force, fraud and boycott against farm labor. It was declared in 1868 that in South Carolina:

The whites do not think it wrong to shoot, stab or knock down Negroes on slight provocation. It is actually thought a great point among certain classes to be able to boast that one has killed or beaten a Negro.[3]

The following resolutions were passed at public meetings of planters in South Carolina:

Resolved, That if inconsistent with views of the authorities to remove the military, we express the opinion that the plan of the military to *compel the freedman* to contract with his former owner, when desired by the latter, is wise, prudent, and absolutely necessary.

Resolved, That we, the planters of the district, pledge ourselves not to contract with

any freedmen unless he can produce a certificate of regular discharge from his former owner.

Resolved, That under no circumstances whatsoever will we rent land to any freedmen, nor will we permit them to live on our premises as employees.[4]

In the Abbeville district of South Carolina it was said:

Here a planter worked nearly one hundred (100) hands near Cokesburg, ten (10) of them on the South Carolina railroad for six (6) months (the planter receiving their wages), and the remainder on his plantation, raising a crop of corn, wheat, rice, cotton, etc. After the crop was harvested the laborers were brought to Charleston, where, being destitute, they had to be rationed by the government. After their arrival in this city the planter distributed fifty dollars ($50) among them. The largest amount any one received was one dollar and twenty-five cents ($1.25) and from that down to fifty cents (50c), some receiving nothing. One peck of dry corn a week was the only ration furnished the farm hands.[5]

Meantime, the growth of sentiment in favor of Negro suffrage was quickened because of the action of South Carolina and other states. Chief Justice Chase visited the state and spoke to the Negroes. He said, "I believe there is not a member of the Government who would not be pleased to see universal suffrage."

The Negroes were already bestirring themselves. In May, 1864, at Port Royal, they held a meeting which elected delegates to the National Union Convention, which was to be held in Baltimore in June. In November, 1865, the colored people met at Zion Church, Charleston,

[3] *Ibid.*, p. 326.

[4] *Congressional Globe*, 39th Congress, 1st Session, Part I, p. 93.

[5] *Report of the Joint Committee on Reconstruction, 1866,* Part II (Abbeville District), p. 225.

and protested against the work of the convention and of the legislature. The legislature refused to receive this petition, and determined to ignore the matter of Negro suffrage entirely. Orr attended the National Union Convention in Philadelphia in 1866, and advised the legislature to reject the Fourteenth Amendment. This the legislature did with only one negative vote in both Houses.

The military commanders, under the Reconstruction legislation, did much to abolish discrimination. One captain of a vessel was fined who refused to allow a colored woman to ride as a first-class passenger, and General Canby, a Kentuckian, whom Johnson appointed in March, 1867, ordered that Negroes serve on juries. This led to excitement and protests.

Northern capitalists began to appear in the state. They were, at first, welcomed:

Men of capital are coming from the North by every steamer in view of investing in cotton and rice. We are glad to see such a lively trade in South Carolina; it benefits everyone.

Later, and especially when they began to take part in politics, they were loaded with every accusation. Some of them were army officers; others, employees of the Freedmen's Bureau; some were farmers, and some religious and educational leaders. The Negroes, naturally, turned to them for leadership and received it. They helped organize the Negroes in Union Leagues in order to teach them citizenship and united action. Northern visitors continued to come. Senator Henry Wilson of Massachusetts spoke at Charleston:

After four bloody years, Liberty triumphed and slavery has died to rise no more. . . . The creed of equal rights, equal privileges and equal immunities for all men in America is hereafter to be the practical policy of the Republic. . . . Never vote unless you vote for the country which made you free. Register your names. Vote for a united country. Vote for the old flag. Vote for a change in the constitution of the state that your liberties may be consummated.

Under the Reconstruction law of 1867, 46,882 whites and 80,550 blacks voted; the planter class refrained from participation in hope that the scheme would fail:

	Whites	Blacks	Total
Total Registration	46,882	80,550	127,432
"For the Convention" .	2,350	66,418	68,768
"Against a Convention"	2,278		2,278
Not Voting	42,354	14,132	56,486
Majority "For a Convention"			66,490

In ten of the thirty-one counties there were white majorities, and in the remaining twenty-one counties, black majorities.

Party conventions began to meet. The first one was that of the Union Republican Party, which met in Charleston with nine county representatives. It adjourned to Columbia, where nineteen counties were represented. It was attended by colored and white men, including some Southern men like Thomas J. Robertson, a wealthy native.

The reaction among the whites led to three parties. Governor Orr and his party accepted the Reconstruction acts, and planned to work with the Negroes. Wade Hampton proposed to accept the acts, but only with the idea of finally dominating the Negro vote and having Negroes follow the lead of their former masters. Hampton owned large plantations in South Carolina and Mississippi.

The New York *Herald* summarized his views as follows: "He appeals to the blacks, lately his slaves, as his political superiors, to try the political experiment of harmonizing with their late white masters before going into the political service of strangers. . . . The broad fact that the two races in the South must henceforth harmonize on a political basis to avoid a bloody conflict is the ground covered by Wade Hampton."

A third party was led by former Governor Perry and Thomas W. Woodward.

"Strange to say," wrote Perry, "there are many persons in the Southern States whose high sense of honor would not let them adopt the Fourteenth Amendment, who are now urging the people to swallow voluntarily the Military Bill, regardless of honor, principle, or consistency." If the state were forced to acquiesce in the tyranny of Congress, he added, "she need not embrace the hideous thing. . . . If we are to wear manacles, let them be put on by our tyrants, not ourselves." He argued the folly of attempting to control the Negro vote. "General Hampton and his friends," he asserted, "had just as well try to control a herd of wild buffaloes as the Negro vote." Woodward was violent in denouncing the compromisers. "Why, oh, why, my Southern nigger worshippers," he cried, "will you grope your way through this worse than Egyptian darkness? Why not cease this crawling on your bellies and assume the upright form of men? . . . Stop, I pray you, your efforts at harmony, your advice about conventions, your pusillanimous insinuations about confiscations, etc., or you will goad these people by flattery to destruction, before they have a chance to pick out the cotton crop."[6]

Perry proposed to appeal to the courts, and advised the whites to register and vote against the constitutional convention. The convention of whites was held a week before the constitutional convention, with twenty-one of the thirty-one

[6] Simkins and Woody, *South Carolina During Reconstruction*, pp. 85–87.

districts represented. This convention made coöperation on the part of Negroes of any intelligence utterly impossible. It declared:

"The fact is patent to all . . . that the Negro is utterly unfitted to exercise the highest function of a citizen. . . . We protest against this subversion of the social order, whereby an ignorant and depraved race is placed in power and influence above the virtuous, the educated, and the refined." The nation was informed that the white people of South Carolina "would never acquiesce in Negro Equality or supremacy." The president of the convention complained that the declarations were filled with adjectives and epithets, which put a weapon in the hands of the enemies of the movement.

The state convention, when it met, had Negro members for the first time in the history of the state. Seventy-six of the one hundred and twenty-four delegates were colored. As in Mississippi and elsewhere, a number of the planter class had early contemplated an effort to control the Negro vote, and thus quickly to get rid of military rule. On the other hand, the Negroes, because of the educated free Negro element, some considerable talent among the slaves, and the influx of Negroes from the North, showed unusual foresight and modesty. The convention was earnest, and on the whole, well-conducted. Of the seventy-six colored men, it is said, fifty-seven had been slaves.

"The native whites felt," said the correspondent of the New York *Times*, "that the destinies of the state were safer in the hands of the unlettered Ethiopians than in those of the whites of the body." "Beyond all question," was the effusive comment of the Charleston *Daily News*, "the best men in the convention are the colored members. Considering the influences under which they were called to-gether, and their imperfect acquaintance with parliamentary law, they have dis-played, for the most part, remarkable moderation and dignity. . . . They have assembled neither to pull wires like some, nor to make money like others; but to legislate for the welfare of the race to which they belong."

There were twenty-seven Southern white members of the convention, some of them honest and earnest, and some of them with questionable antecedents. One of them had made up a purse to buy a cane for Brooks, after he had assaulted Sumner; another had assisted in hauling down the Union flag from Fort Sumter; a third had been a slave trader. Among the Northerners were colored and white men of education and character, as well as some adventurers.

To the chagrin of many white onlook-ers, the convention was not a disorderly group; "the delegates did not create 'the Negro bedlam' which tradition has asso-ciated with them. President Mackey said that he had 'no unpleasant reminiscences of those acrimonious bickerings which, in all deliberative assemblies, are often in-cidental to the excitement of debate and the attrition of antagonistic minds.' "[7] There was no tendency to insult the white South, and even deference was paid to the defeated Confederate soldiers.

This was in striking contrast to the wild and unscrupulous attacks made by the press upon this convention. Some called the experiment "the maddest, most unscrupulous, and infamous revolution in history," and said that it was snatching power from the hands of the race that settled the country and transferring it to its former slaves, an "ignorant and feeble race."

The representative of one paper was expelled from the floor for sneering at the "ringed, striped, and streaked conven-tion." Other papers received all possible courtesies.

The real basis of opposition to the new régime was economic. Nothing showed this clearer than one fact, and that is that the chief and repeated accusation against the convention and succeeding legislatures was that they were composed of poor men, white and black. The white 47 delegates were said to have paid alto-gether $761 in annual taxes, of which one conservative paid $508. The total taxes paid by the 74 Negroes were $117, of which a Charleston Negro paid $85. Twenty-three of the whites and fifty-nine of the colored paid no taxes whatever. . . .[8]

When the convention opened, ex-Governor Orr was invited to address them. In his speech he stressed the fact that the freedmen needed education, and that they did not represent the intelli-gence nor wealth of the state, and he recommended limited suffrage, a home-stead law and education.

The plight of debtors after the losses and changes of war brought much debate in the constitutional convention. A white delegate advocated a three months' mora-torium on debt collections, and a colored member supported the proposal. But Cardozo, a colored man, and later the Treasurer of the State, said:

I am opposed to the passage of this resolu-tion. The convention should be certain of the constitutionality of their acts. The law of the United States does not allow a state to pass a law impairing the obligations of con-tracts. This, I think, is therefore a proper sub-ject for the judiciary. I am heartily in favor of relief, but I wish the convention to have nothing to do with the matter.

[8] *Ku Klux Conspiracy, South Carolina,* Part 2, pp. 1238–1250.

[7] *Ibid.,* p. 105.

R. G. DeLarge, a colored delegate, afterward Land Commissioner, said:

It has been said in opposition to this measure, that the proposed legislation was for a certain class; however, no gentlemen can rise and argue that the proposed measure is for the benefit of any specific class. I hold in my hands letters from almost every section of the state addressed to members of the convention, crying out for relief. These letters depict in strong language the impoverished condition of the people, and demand that something should be done to relieve them. I deny in toto that this is a piece of class legislation, and I believe nothing but the zeal of the member who spoke yesterday induced them to speak of it as such. It is simply a request to General Canby to relieve the necessities of a large part of the people of the state. Some members have gone farther, and said it was a shame to keep the freedmen from becoming purchasers and owners of land. . . .

It has been argued that the execution of the laws compelling the sale of the lands will benefit the poor man by affording him an opportunity to get possession of the lands. That argument, I am confident, cannot be sustained. If they are sold, they will be sold at public sale, and sold in immense tracts, just as they are at present. They will pass into the hands of the merciless speculators, who will never allow the poor man to get an inch without first drawing his life's blood in payment. The poor freedmen are the poorest of poor and unprepared to purchase lands. The poor whites are not in condition to purchase lands. The facts are, the poor class are clamoring, and their voices have been voiced far beyond the limits of South Carolina, away to the seat of the government, appealing for assistance and relief from actual starvation.

The problem of the land came in for early consideration. The landless, it was felt, should be aided in the acquirement of property and the landed aristocracy discriminated against. It was proposed that Congress be petitioned to lend the state one million dollars to be used in the purchase of land for the colored people; that the legislature be required to appoint a land commission; and that homesteads up to a certain value be exempt from the levy of processes.

One must view this action in light of what had taken place with regard to land in South Carolina. When Northern forces captured Port Royal in November, 1861, the Federal authorities took over 195 plantations and employed over 10,000 former slaves in raising cotton. Early in 1862, they imported labor superintendents from the North, and organized the enterprise. In July, 1862, Congress laid a direct tax on the land of the states in rebellion. When the absentee landholders of Port Royal failed to pay, their plantations were sold at public auction to satisfy a part of the debt of $363,570 which had been imposed upon South Carolina. Considerable other property, which was regarded as abandoned, was seized in Charleston. The lands that were auctioned off were bought largely by Northerners, although a few Negroes who had got hold of a little money from their labor bought certain plantations.

On January 16, 1868, General Sherman issued his celebrated Field Order, Number 15. All the Sea Islands, from Charleston to Port Royal, and adjoining lands to the distance of thirty miles inland, were set aside for the use of the Negroes who had followed his army. General Saxton executed this order, and divided 485,000 acres of land among 40,000 Negroes. They were given, however, only possessory titles, and in the end, the government broke its implied promise and drove them off the land.

In the convention, the whole matter of land for the landless came up for considerable debate. Cardozo said that he did not believe in the confiscation of property, but since slavery was gone, the plantation system must go with it. Whipper, another colored man, was more inclined to protect the interests of the planters, and reminded the members that they were representatives of all classes in the community and not simply of a particular class.

This debate on the economic situation was prolonged. All contracts and liabilities for the purchase of slaves, where the money had not yet been paid, were annulled. J. J. Wright, colored, and later a state Supreme Court judge, said of this measure:

I know it is said by our opponents that we are an unlawful assembly, and that we are an unconstitutional body. I know we are here under the laws of Congress, lawfully called together for the discharge of certain duties, and the repudiation of debts contracted for slaves. . . .
It is the duty of the convention to do what? It is our duty to destroy all elements of the institution of slavery. If we do not, we recognize the right of property in man.

A homestead law to the value of $1,000 in real estate and $500 in personal property was passed. Rainey declared that Congress would probably never pass an act confiscating the land, but the other colored members, including Ransier, wanted to petition Congress for a loan of a million dollars to purchase land.

A colored delegate said on this matter:

My colleague presented a petition asking the Congress of the United States to appropriate one million dollars for a specific purpose — to purchase homesteads for the people of South Carolina; not the colored people, as the gentleman from Barnwell has attempted to prove, but to all, irrespective of color. He has also attempted to prove that the money cannot be obtained, but has failed to carry conviction to the minds of any of the members. There is plenty of land in the state that can be purchased for two dollars an acre, and one million will buy us five hundred thousand acres; cut this into small farms of twenty acres and we have twenty-five thousand farms. Averaging seven persons to a family that twenty acres can sustain, and we have one hundred and seventy-five thousand persons, men, women and children, who for a million dollars will be furnished means of support; that is, one-fourth of the entire people of the state.

Mr. R. C. DeLarge, colored, continued on the same subject:

There are over one thousand freedmen in this state who, within the last year, purchased lands from the native whites on the same terms. We propose that the government should aid us in the purchase of more lands, to be divided into small tracts and given on the above-mentioned credit to homeless families to cultivate for their support. It is well-known that in every district the freedmen are roaming from one side to the other, not because they expect to get land, but because the large landholders are not able to employ them, and will not sell their lands unless the freedmen have the cash to pay for them. These are facts that cannot be contradicted by the gentleman from Barnwell. I know one large landholder in Colleton District who had twenty-one freedmen working for him upon his plantation the entire year. He raised a good crop but the laborers have not succeeded in getting any reimbursement for their labor. They are now roaming to Charleston and back, trying to get remuneration for their services. We propose to give them lands, and to place them in a position by which they will be enabled to sustain themselves.
In doing this, we will add to the depleted treasury of the state, and the large plantation system of the country will be broken up. The large plantation will be divided into small farms, giving support to more people and yielding more taxes to the state. It will bring out the whole resources of the state. I desire it to be distinctly understood that I do not

advocate this measure simply for the benefit of my own race.

After much discussion by various white members on the same subject, Mr. F. L. Cardozo, colored, voiced the thought of colored men who demanded that the government furnish land for the freedmen:

The poor freedmen were induced, by many Congressmen even, to expect confiscation. They held out the hope of confiscation. General Sherman did confiscate; gave the lands to the freedmen; and if it were not for President Johnson, they would have them now. The hopes of the freedmen have not been realized, and I do not think that asking for a loan of one million, to be paid by a mortgage upon the land, will be half as bad as has been supposed. I have been told by the Assistant Commissioner that he has been doing on a private scale what this petition proposes. I say every opportunity of helping the colored people should be seized upon. We should certainly vote for some measure of relief for the colored men, as we have to the white men who mortgaged their property to perpetuate slavery, and whom they have liberated from their bonds.

Mr. W. J. Whipper, colored, was more conservative, and only wanted protection from immediate monopoly:

The present owners will be compelled before long to sell portions of their land, and sell them to freedmen or whoever can pay for them. But if sold now, they will be sold in large bodies, or large tracts, so that nobody but a capitalist will be able to buy.

This demand for land was characterized as demagoguery by the property holders, but land was, as many speakers suggested, the economic means of raising the level of the electorate. A petition was passed by a great majority, asking Congress to appropriate funds for buying land. But Senator Wilson replied that

this was impractical, and the convention, thereupon, created a state commission for buying lands and selling them to the freedmen.

The convention attacked race discrimination squarely. A colored man, Dr. B. F. Randolph, offered the following amendment: "Distinction on account of race or color in any case whatever shall be prohibited, and all classes of citizens, irrespective of race and color, shall enjoy all common, equal, and political privileges." He said:

It is, doubtless, the impression of the members of the convention that the Bill of Rights as it stands secures perfect political and legal equality to all the people of South Carolina. It is a fact, however, that nowhere is it laid down in the instrument, emphatically and definitely, that all the people of the state, irrespective of race and color, shall enjoy equal privileges. Our forefathers were no doubt anti-slavery men, and they intended that slavery should die out. Consequently, the word color is not to be found in the Constitution or Declaration of Independence. On the contrary, it stated "all men are created free and equal." In our Bill of Rights, I want to settle the question forever by making the meaning so plain that a wayfaring man, though a fool, cannot misunderstand it. The majority of the people of South Carolina, who are rapidly becoming property-holders, are colored citizens — the descendants of the African race — who have been ground down by three hundred years of degradation, and now that the opportunity is afforded, let them be protected by their political rights. The words proposed as an amendment were not calculated to create distinction, but to destroy distinction, and since the Bill of Rights did not declare equality, irrespective of race or color, it was important that they should be inserted.

Thus, discriminations of race and color were abolished by the constitution, and practical application was attempted in the case of the public schools, and the militia.

The convention framed the most liberal provisions for the right of suffrage that any of the Southern constitutions provided. They did not attempt, as in Virginia, Alabama, and Mississippi, to restrict the voting of whites further than was provided by the Reconstruction acts. Indeed, Whipper, a colored delegate, wished to petition Congress to remove all political disabilities from the white citizens. In this Cardozo and Nash agreed, and the motion was passed.

Of course, they made no distinction in race and color. The rights of women were enlarged. The property of married women could not be sold for their husbands' debts, and for the first time in its history, the state was given a divorce law.

Education was discussed at length, and a free common school system voted for. "It is sufficient to say here that for the first time the fundamental law of the state carried the obligation of universal education and demanded the creation of a school system like that of Northern states."[9] Nothing that the convention did aroused more opposition among property-holding whites. In the first place, as a white woman told a Northern teacher:

I do assure you that you might as well try to teach your horse or mule to read as to teach these niggers.[10]

In the second place, the whites calculated that the school system would cost $900,000 a year, and that the new taxation would fall upon them.

In the debate on the school system, there was not a moment's hesitation, but there was considerable difference of opinion as to whether education should be made compulsory or not.

R. C. DeLarge, colored, said in the debate, "The schools may be open to all, but to declare that parents shall send their children to them whether they are willing or not is, in my judgment, going a step beyond the bounds of prudence. Is there any logic or reason in inserting in the constitution a provision which cannot be enforced?"

Mr. A. J. Ransier, colored, said, "I am sorry to differ with my colleague from Charleston on this question. I contend that in proportion to the education of the people so is their progress in civilization. Believing this, I believe that the committee has properly provided for the compulsory education of all children in this state between the ages named in the section."

Mr. J. A. Chesnut, colored, spoke on separation in schools:

Has not this convention the right to establish a free school system for the poorer classes? Then if there be a hostile disposition among the whites, an unwillingness to send their children to school, the fault is their own, not ours. Look at the idle youth around us. Is the sight not enough to invigorate every man with a desire to do something to remove this vast weight of ignorance that presses the masses down? I have no desire to curtail the privileges of freedmen, but when we look at the opportunities neglected, even by the whites of South Carolina, I must confess that I am more than ever disposed to compel parents, especially of my own race, to send their children to school. If the whites object to it, let it be so.

Mr. F. L. Cardozo said,

It was argued by some yesterday with some considerable weight that we should do everything in our power to incorporate in the constitution all possible measures that will

9 Simkins and Woody, *South Carolina During Reconstruction*, p. 100.
10 *Ibid.*, p. 424.

conciliate those opposed to us. No one would go further in conciliating others than I would. But we should be careful of what we do to conciliate.

In the first place, there is an element that is opposed to us no matter what we do, which will never be conciliated. It is not that they are opposed so much to the constitution we may frame, but they are opposed to us sitting in the convention. Their objection is of such a radical and fundamental nature, that any attempt to frame a constitution to please them would be abortive.

In the next place, there are those who are doubtful; and gentlemen here say if we frame a constitution to suit these parties, they will come over to our side. They are only waiting to see whether or not it will be successful.

Then there is the third class who honestly question our capacity to frame a constitution. I respect that class, and believe if we do justice to them, laying our corner-stone on a sure foundation of republican government and liberal principles, the intelligence of that class will be conciliated, and they are worthy of conciliation.

Before I proceed to discuss the question, I want to divest it of all false issue of the imaginary consequences that some gentlemen have illogically thought will result from the adoption of this section with the word "compulsory." They affirm that it compels the attendance of both white and colored children in the same schools. There is nothing of the kind in the section. It simply says that all the children shall be educated; but how, it is left with the parents to decide. It is left to the parent to say whether the child should be sent to a public or private school. There can be separate schools for white and colored. It is left so that if any colored child wishes to go to a white school, it shall have the privilege of doing so. I have no doubt, in most localities colored people will prefer separate schools, particularly until some of the present prejudice against their race is removed.

The committee proposed that persons coming of age after 1875 must be able to read and write before voting, but Cardozo opposed it because he said it would take more than ten years and a great deal of money to complete the system, and he wanted to extend the time to 1890. Three other colored members spoke against any qualification, and it was, therefore, stricken out.

To bridge over the interval before the state school system could be installed, Mr. B. F. Randolph, colored, presented the following petition, which was referred to the Committee on Miscellaneous Provisions of the Constitution: "We, the undersigned, people of South Carolina, in convention assembled, do hereby recommend that the Bureau of Refugees, Freedmen and Abandoned Lands be continued until the restoration of civil authority; that then a Bureau of Education be established, in order that an efficient system of schools be established."

"Perhaps the convention's achievement of greatest permanent importance was the reform of local and judicial administration."[11]

Judicial circuits were to be called counties, and some new counties were arranged. A Court of Probate was established in each county, and justices of the peace were given wider jurisdiction. Judges were to be elected, instead of appointed, and in spite of much criticism, the new system worked well. From 1870 to 1877 the Supreme Court was composed of a Negro, a native Southerner, and a Northerner. Its administration was fair and its decisions just. Most of the circuit judges were native whites and honest men. Mixed juries were the rule, and no fault was found with them. They did not hesitate to convict colored prisoners. The trial judges came in for the greatest criticism. Among them were

11 *Ibid.*, p. 101.

numbers of ignorant and unqualified persons, and there was a good deal of misappropriation of fees and costs. On the other hand, it was difficult to get proper trial judges, because so many qualified whites refused to serve.

Wright, the Negro who was on the Supreme Court, was the first colored man admitted to the bar in Pennsylvania. He had been connected with the Freedmen's Bureau; then became a member of the constitutional convention, and a state senator. He was elected to the bench in February, 1870, to fill out an unexpired term, and was re-elected in December, 1870, for the full term. He resigned under Hampton in August, 1877.

Although he lisped, Wright was a good speaker, decidedly intelligent, and generally said to be the best fitted colored man in the state for the position.

Some reforms were made in the county government. Most of the officers were to be elected by popular vote, and boards of commissioners were appointed for the highways, and for collection and disbursement of taxes.

Some of the delegates wanted to legislate concerning wages, which caused great indignation among the planters. It was suggested, for instance, that planters be required to pay back wages from the time of the issue of the Emancipation Proclamation, and that the division of one-half of the crop for tenant farmers be made compulsory. Such legislation was inherently just and reasonable but fifty years too early for public opinion in any modern country.

Among other things, the constitution abolished imprisonment for debt, and dueling, and did away with property qualifications, for voting or holding office. The colored members, despite their inexperience, gave evidence, here and there, of care and thrift. For instance,

when the question of the pay of members of the convention came up, a discussion arose. Mr. L. S. Langley moved that the pay per diem of $12 in bills receivable be laid on the table. J. J. Wright moved that $10 be inserted. N. G. Parker, white, moved to fix the pay at $11. C. P. Leslie, colored, demurred: "I desire to say a word before that resolution be passed, and be put right on record. I am perfectly willing to receive $3 per day in greenbacks for my services. I think that sum all they are worth, and further, if I got any more, it would be so much more than I have been in the habit of receiving, I might possibly go on a spree and lose the whole of it. Now I ask any of the delegates in this body if they were called upon to pay a similar body of men out of their pockets, how much they would be willing to pay each member. I will stake my existence on it they would not pay more than $1.50 per day to each member. I want to be recorded as always being opposed to a high tariff, but not against any reasonable compensation. But this eight or nine dollars a day, when we consider all the surroundings and conditions of the people, looks too much like a fraud."

The new constitution for South Carolina was adopted by the Convention in April, 1868. It was eventually adopted by the people — 70,000 voting for it, 27,000 against it, and 35,000 abstaining.

The constitution was written in good English and was an excellent document, "embodying some of the best legal principles of the age. In letter it was as good as any other constitution the state has ever had, or as most American states had at that time. This assertion is supported by the practical endorsement which a subsequent generation of South Carolinians gave it; the conservative whites were content to live under it for eighteen years after they recovered control of the state government, and when in 1895 they met to make a new constitution, the document they produced had many of the features of the constitution of 1868.". . .[12]

The first governor, under the new régime, was Robert K. Scott, born in Pennsylvania, a colonel of Union troops during the war, and assistant commissioner of the Freedmen's Bureau. Scott faced great difficulties, and is generally conceded to have been a well-meaning man. A well-born native Southern white was Franklin J. Moses, Jr. His father had been a prominent South Carolinian, Senator before the war, and was respected by all people. Moses married the daughter of a distinguished Southerner; was private secretary to one of the former Governors, and became a lawyer and an editor in favor of Johnson's Reconstruction. When the Reconstruction acts were passed he went over to the side of the carpetbaggers and Negroes; he took a prominent part in the constitutional convention, and afterward became Speaker of the House, and in 1872, Governor. He was denounced as unscrupulous and dishonest, and extravagant in his manner of living.

The colored leaders formed a very interesting group. Francis L. Cardozo was free-born of Negro, Jewish and Indian descent. He was educated at the University of Glasgow, and in London, and went to New Haven, where he served as a Presbyterian minister. After the war, he came to Charleston and was Principal of Avery Institute. He was secretary of state during 1868–1872, and treasurer of the state during 1872–1876. He was a handsome, well-groomed man, with cultivated manners, and honest in official life. He was accused in several instances,

[12] *Ibid.,* pp. 93–94.

but no dishonest act was ever proven against him.

Joseph H. Rainey was the first Negro to represent South Carolina in the House of Representatives. Robert Brown Elliott, born in Massachusetts, was educated at Eton College, in England. He was a first-rate lawyer; served in the legislature, and was twice elected to Congress. He had a commanding presence, and a fine gift of oratory. Richard A. Cain was a leader, and afterward bishop in the A.M.E. Church. His paper, *The Missionary Record,* was the most influential Negro paper in South Carolina. He served in the Senate and two terms in Congress. Robert C. DeLarge was a tailor from Charleston, and had been an agent in the Freedmen's Bureau. He served in the legislature, and while his education was limited, he had large influence. Beverly Nash had been a slave before the war, and afterward a waiter. When grown he learned to read and write, and became an earnest and hard-working leader.

Alonzo J. Ransier was elected lieutenant-governor in 1870. He was a free Negro, and became a member of the constitutional convention of the legislature, and auditor of Charleston County. In 1872, he went to Congress. He made a good presiding officer of the state senate, being dignified and alert. Richard H. Gleaves was lieutenant-governor in 1872–1876. He was from Pennsylvania, and had acted as probate judge. He was intelligent and knew parliamentary law. Samuel J. Lee was a Negro Speaker of the House, in 1872–1874. He was born in the state, worked as a farmer and laborer in lumber mills, and was self-educated. He was polished and a good lawyer. Stephen A. Swailes, a colored man of Pennsylvania, was a Union soldier, and school-teacher. He became a senator, and was known for his integrity and ability as a speaker. Robert Smalls was the one who stole the Confederate ship *Planter* and delivered it to the Union authorities. He was self-educated and popular. He was a member of Congress until after Reconstruction. These men were all poor and doubtless some of them accepted bribes and shared in graft. But very few of them were thoroughly venal or purchasable against their convictions. When it came to personal favors or sharing in gifts and gains which followed legislation of which they honestly approved, some of them were certainly approachable.

Negroes were conspicuous members of the legislatures. "There was a large proportion of former slaves, and at first perhaps two-thirds of them could not write, but by 1871, most of them had learned at least to read and write. Many of them were speakers of force and eloquence,

while others were silent or crude. In the Senate, it was said that some of the colored members spoke exceedingly well, with great ease and grace of manners. Others, were awkward and coarse."[13]

One observer recorded that "The President of the Senate and the Speaker of the House, both colored, were elegant and accomplished men, highly educated, who would have creditably presided over any commonwealth's legislative assembly."

"The majority of the voters of the state were Negroes, and in every session but one that race had a majority in the legislature. They outnumbered, and in many cases outshone, their carpetbag and scalawag contemporaries."[14]

In the first legislature there were 127 members, of whom 87 were colored, and 40 white. According to the available figures, the composition of Reconstruction legislatures in South Carolina seems to have been as follows:[15]

	Senate		House		Total		
	Negroes	Whites	Negroes	Whites	Negroes	Whites	Total
1868–1869	10	21	78	46	88	67	155
1870–1871	10	20	75	49	85	69	154
1872–1873	16	17	80	42	96	59	155
1874–1875	16	17	61	63	77	80	157
1876–1878	4	14	58	64	62	78	130

It will be seen from these figures that the white members of the legislature, from their control of the Senate, were always able to block Negro legislators; and that Negro control of the legislature was only possible because most of the white Senators voted with the Negroes. In the legislature of 1874, the whites had a majority in both Houses. It can hardly be said, therefore, that the Negroes of South Carolina had absolute control of the state at any time.

The economic status of the legislature of 1870–1871 is shown by their given

occupations: 10 lawyers, 31 farmers, 9 physicians, 17 clergymen, 12 teachers, 16 planters, 13 merchants, 3 merchant tailors, 3 clerks, 2 masons, 8 builders, 1 engineer, 1 marble dealer, 8 carpenters, 2 hotel keepers, 1 druggist, 1 bookkeeper,

13 *Ibid.*, pp. 128–129.

14 *Ibid.*, p. 128.

15 These figures are from Taylor, Simkins and Woody, and Work's compilation in the *Journal of Negro History*, V, p. 63. Simkins and Woody's figures have many inaccuracies and the figures of Taylor and Work are incomplete. Compare also Reynolds, *Reconstruction in South Carolina*.

1 wheelwright, 4 coachmakers, 1 tanner, 2 mechanics, 1 chemist, 1 auditor, 1 hatter, 1 blacksmith, 1 tailor.

The state sent seven Negroes to Congress; made two of them lieutenant-governors; and for four years, two of them were speakers of the House. One was secretary of state and treasurer of the state. Another was adjutant and inspector general. These men were of various colors and mixtures of blood, and there was a good deal of difference of opinion, as to whether the mulattoes or the full-blooded blacks were superior. But one observer asserted that "the colored men generally were superior in decency and ability to the majority of the native white Radical legislators."[16] And another said that "the quadroons and octoroons of the Senate are infinitely superior in personal appearance to their white Yankee and native compeers."[17]

Most of these men had been slaves, although a few of them were well-educated. They had ability, and in some cases, more than ordinary ability. But above all, they were in the midst of a mighty social and economic change, and were swayed by the social and political revolution around them. "The bottom rail was on the top," and the former ruling oligarchy was now displaced by those who represented neither the wealth nor the traditions of the state.

The bitterness of this campaign against the Reconstruction governments was almost inconceivable.

One unfamiliar with the situation would think the editors and their correspondents had gone crazy with anger or were obsessed with some fearful mania, so great was the ridicule, contempt, and obloquy showered upon the representatives of the state. With the deepest scorn for a scalawag, with all the Southern hatred for an adventuring Yankee, and with either sympathy or shame for the ignorant, misled Negro, the press, the aristocracy, the poor whites, the up-country, the low-country — all with one voice protested against the "unlawful assembly" in Columbia maintained in power, they said, by the Federal bayonet. The Fairfield *Herald* battled "against the hell-born policy which has trampled the fairest and noblest States of our great sisterhood beneath the unholy hoofs of African savages and shoulder-strapped brigands — the policy which has given up millions of our free-born, high-souled brethren and sisters, countrymen and countrywomen of Washington, Rutledge, Marion, and Lee, to the rule of gibbering, louse-eaten, devil-worshiping barbarians, from the jungles of Dahomey, and peripatetic buccaneers from Cape Cod, Memphremagog, Hell, and Boston.[18]

A new system of taxation came in with the Reconstruction government. It provided for a uniform rate of assessment on all property at its full value. This was a departure from the system previous to the war, which put a low valuation on land and slaves and heavy taxation on merchants, professions and banking. The merchant before the war paid five or six times as great a rate of taxation as the planter. In 1859, the total tax value of lands in the state was $10,257,000, while lots and buildings in Charleston were valued at $22,274,000. The tax on all the land of the state averaged less than five cents an acre in 1860. When the new system came in, it was difficult to find persons to administer it and every landholder objected to it.

The new system met all sorts of opposi-

16 *News,* March 17, 1870, in Simkins and Woody, *South Carolina During Reconstruction,* p. 130.

17 *News,* March 10, 1871, in Simkins and Woody, *South Carolina During Reconstruction,* p. 130.

18 Simkins and Woody, *South Carolina During Reconstruction,* pp. 121–122.

tion from unsympathetic administrators and the newspapers of the state. Governor Scott expected $300,000,000 worth of property as a basis of taxation, but less than $115,000,000 were returned. This the Board of Equalization raised to $180,000,000. As the assessments decreased, the rate of taxation increased. The total assessment in 1869 was $181,000,000, and in 1877, under Hampton, $101,000,000. As the average rate of taxes rose, the property holders said that the Negro government wanted to raise taxes so as to confiscate the land.

The new government could not collect the tax levied. It met an organized and bitter boycott of property. In 1868, $175,688 of assessed tax was uncollected; in 1869, $248,165, and in 1870, $524,026 — a total of nearly a million dollars in three years. Part of this delinquency was due to real poverty; but part was due to deliberate obstruction on the part of property holders. Taxation had to be increased to cover delinquency and to meet new expenses. In 1860, taxation on a half billion of property was $1,280,383; in 1870, $2,767,675 was assessed on $183,000,000. The increase of taxation was partly accounted for by gradually increased expenditures for education, construction, and charitable institutions.

At the same time, the inflation of the currency makes comparison with conditions previous to the war difficult. More money was certainly raised by the state during Reconstruction. But, on the other hand, a much larger proportion of the expenditures was designed to aid the laboring poor, and did aid them largely. Indeed, it might have changed the whole economic position of the proletariat if it had been efficiently and honestly expended.

In the legislature in 1868, the free common school system was organized tempo-

rarily, and permanently in 1870. Relief was extended to various classes of citizens, especially poor laborers. In 1868 and 1869, an act was passed providing for a land commissioner, who was to act under a board. Land was to be purchased in various parts of the state, and was to be sold in plots of not less than twenty-five and not more than one hundred acres to actual settlers. Two hundred thousand dollars' worth of bonds were provided to finance this proposal, and later this was increased to $500,000. The land commissioner was to hold office at the pleasure of an Advisory Board, consisting of chief state officers.

One of the chief sources of corruption in nearly all the reconstructed states was railroad building. And the reasons for this are easily misconceived because of the changed economic status of railroads today. It must be remembered that at the beginning throughout the country and the world, the railroad was a public highway, and for this reason a public enterprise toward whose building and maintenance the public rightly contributed. It was only after the railroad was built and established by public funds, that private interests monopolized it and sequestered its income to make individual millionaires.

In the South, the railroads had lagged. The planters would not submit to public taxation, and they would not divert funds from their private luxury consumption, in order to furnish capital. South Carolina was particularly a case in point. Charleston, by all rules of commerce, should have been one of the great ports of the United States. It was a gateway to the West; it should have at least connected its own uplands with the coast, and it might have tapped the West through Cincinnati, and the great cotton belt through the Southern South. But efforts toward this end before the war had but small success.

It was perfectly natural that the first thought of those who were reconstructing the state should turn toward railroad building as a means of economic rehabilitation. The usual method was the old one of loaning credit of the state. It meant, not that the state invested money, but simply that the state permitted the issue of bonds and guaranteed the payment of interest and principal. On a sound economic proposition, conducted by honest men, this was simply a way of securing private capital for a semi-public enterprise, which would greatly increase the prosperity of the state.

Railway mileage in South Carolina had increased from 289 to 973, between 1850–1860. By 1865, there were 1,007 miles. Then construction practically stopped, and effort was turned toward rebuilding the railroads and giving them new equipment.

The difficulty was that a flock of cormorants whose business was cheating and manipulation in the issue and sale of bonds and other certificates of enterprise, moved first West and then South, and took charge of railroad promotion. They were largely Northern financiers, in some cases already discredited in the centers of finance and driven out of the overworked investment fields North and West. They came South with an address and a technique which only trained, experienced, and honest administrators could have withstood. They flaunted the chances of quick and easy money before the faces of ruined planters, small Northern investors, and the few Negroes who had some little capital. The result was widespread graft, debt and corruption in South Carolina and North Carolina, in Florida and Georgia, in Louisiana, and in other states.

There was, however, in the reorganization, for instance, of the Greenville and Columbia Railroad, nothing worse than the ordinary stock-jobbing enterprise common all over the nation; and prominent Southerners, like ex-Governor Orr and J. P. Reed, were concerned in it. Instead of concentrating efforts on the rebuilding of the railroad and its equipment, most of the time and energy was spent in seeking to market stock in New York. This failed and the road was bankrupt by the end of the Reconstruction era, just as it was at the beginning.

In the same way, the Blue Ridge road, backed not only by carpetbaggers but by leading white Southerners, was prostrate after the war and sued for state aid. The legislature authorized aid in 1868, but the contract for rebuilding demanded much more money than the bonds provided for. Eventually the road was sold to a private company composed as usual not only of carpetbaggers but of planters. Matters were so manipulated that a state contingent liability of $4,000,000 of bonds was transmuted into an actual state indebtedness of $1,800,000. Again little was done actually to restore the road, and the company went into bankruptcy.

Thus in most cases, bankrupt corporations bequeathed to the Reconstruction régime by ante-bellum organizers, came before the Legislature to secure capital for rebuilding, and then fell into the hands of speculators who tried to make money out of the stock, rather than out of the rebuilding of the road; and these speculators were largely men trained in shady finance in Wall Street, and helped by much of the best element of the Southerners in South Carolina, as well as by the new carpetbag capitalists.

This was a difficult situation, calling for blame and criticism, but to place the blame of it mainly upon the Negro voter and the Negro laborer is a fantastic distortion of the truth. The money misused went primarily to Northern promoters and Southern white administrators. And while, of course, a poverty-stricken electorate was gripped and bribed by such organized thieves, the remedy for this was not the disfranchisement of labor but its education, and such an increased share of the product of industry as to make life livable, without theft or sale of soul.

The appropriations to meet the new expenses had to grow. The fact is that South Carolina had been a state absolutely dominated by landed property. It is said that the ante-bellum state was ruled by 180 great landlords. They had made the functions of the state just as few as possible, and did by private law and on private plantations most of the things which in other states were carried on by the local and state governments. The economic revolution, therefore, which universal suffrage envisaged for this state, was perhaps greater than in any other Southern state. It was for this reason that the right of the masses to vote was so bitterly assailed, and expenditures for the new functions of the state denounced as waste and extravagance.

The result of all this had to be increased taxation. The rate of taxation in 1868–1872 was 9 mills; in 1872–1876 over 11 mills. Yet this was excessive only by comparison with the past and because of recent severe losses. In Northern states, like Illinois, Massachusetts, New York and Pennsylvania, the average was 21½ mills on the dollar.

The grip of poverty was on the South and poverty always is felt most poignantly by those to whom poverty has been unknown. The planters, used to ease and a certain degree of luxury, were the ones that felt the new poverty as a terrible, heaven-shattering thing. They looked upon any action as justifiable if it restored to them the income which they had lost.

On the other hand, both the poor whites and the Negroes were not only poverty-stricken, but, for that reason, peculiarly susceptible to petty graft and bribery. Economically, they had always been stripped bare; a little cash was a curiosity, and a few dollars a fortune. The sale of their votes and political influence was therefore, from the first, simply a matter of their knowledge and conception of what the vote was for and what it could procure. With experience, their conception of its value rose until some of them conceived the idea of making the ballot a power by which they could change their social and economic status, and live like human beings. But before most of them rose to this conception, there were thousands to whom their vote and petty office-holding were simply a means of adding to their small incomes. And when one considers that this was a day when the line between using political power for personal advantage and using it for social uplift was dim and difficult to follow throughout the whole nation, the wonder is that the labor vote of South Carolina so easily ranged itself behind the new school system, the orphanages, the land distribution, and the movements toward reform in public efficiency.

The ascendancy of property over labor and the suffrage was in this day openly maintained by bribery, and if this had been uncommon in the pre-war South, it was simply because universal suffrage had not been established and capital ruled by social sanction rather than by money. In the new situation, property began systematically to attack labor in two ways: First, it deliberately encouraged extravagance, graft and bribery, so as to hasten the downfall of the labor régime. And secondly, it utterly upset the credit of the state, so as to prevent the new state from importing capital.

The failure of taxation to raise the required revenue compelled the state to borrow, and here it fell into the hands of Northern money sharks and Southern repudiators. The state debt October 1, 1867, was $8,378,255. The Constitutional Convention of 1868 repudiated $3,000,000 of this as a Confederate debt, and made the total debt $5,407,306. From this beginning, the state debt increased to $10,665,908 in 1871, while committees claimed that there was evidence of total liabilities outstanding to the amount of 15 or even 30 millions.

The exact amount of the debt was not known; the figures from the reports of the treasurer, comptroller-general, and financial agent did not agree; and it was claimed by the opposition press and even by some of the state officials that there were large issues of fraudulent bonds on the market, and that certain of the state officials had profited thereby.

While the Conservative press continually reviled the Radical government, on no topic was it so prolific or bitter as that of finances and taxation.[19]

The total debt, bonded and contingent, seems to have been:

1860	$12,027,090
1865	15,892,946
1868	14,896,040
1871	22,480,914

In this case, the total indebtedness in 1871 is not clear. The Governor's report makes it a little less than twelve million, but the investigation committee insists that because the state government had

[19] *Ibid.*, pp. 154-155.

printed and issued certain bonds, the amount of which was not definitely known, it was possible that the state might eventually be liable for thirty million dollars.

This did not mean, as many assume, that the state officials received or squandered any such sums. The methods by which small amounts of actual cash received became a paper debt of huge amounts is explained in the Governor's special message of January 9, 1865.

In the fall of 1868, I visited New York City for the purpose of borrowing money on the credit of the state on coupon bonds, under the provisions of the acts of August 26, 1868. I had the assistance of Mr. H. H. Kimpton, United States Senator F. A. Sawyer, and Mr. George S. Cameron. I called at several of the most prominent banking houses to effect the negotiation of the required loan, and they refused to advance any money upon our state securities, for those securities had been already branded with the threat of a speedy repudiation by the political opponents of the administration, who have ever since howled the same cry against the state credit. As the persons who made this threat controlled the press of the state, they were enabled to impress capitalists abroad with the false idea of a speedy reaction that would soon place them again in authority.

As the capitalists well knew that these persons when in power in 1862 did repudiate their debts due Northern creditors, their distrust of our bonds was very natural and apparently well-founded. It soon became evident to every man familiar with our financial standing in New York that to negotiate the loan authorized, the question was not what we would take for the bonds, but what we could get for them. After much effort, and the most judicious management, I succeeded in borrowing money, through Mr. Cameron, at the rate of four dollars in bonds for one dollar in currency, the bonds being rated at 75 per cent below their par value, or at 25 cents on the dollar. This loan, however, was only effected at the extravagant rate of 1½ per cent per month, or 18 per cent a year — a rate only demanded on the most doubtful paper, to cover what is deemed a great risk — for the money loaned.

Subsequent loans were effected at a higher valuation of the bonds, but at the rates of interest varying from 15 to 20 per cent, in addition to commissions necessarily to be paid the financial agent. If, then, $3,200,000 in money has cost the state $9,514,000 in bonds, it does not, therefore, follow that the financial board has criminally conspired against the credit of the state, and still less, that any one member of the board can justly be held up to public execration or stigmatized by an accusation of "high crimes and misdemeanors" for the assumed results of its action. It is proper that I should add that the armed violence which has prevailed in this state for the past three years has had upon our bonds the same effect as actual war in lessening their purchasing-value, as money is dearer in war than in peace. Ku-Kluxism made capitalists shrink from touching the bonds of this state, as a man would shrink from touching a pestilential body.[20]

If there were outstanding in 1874 twenty or even thirty millions of evidences of debt, it is unlikely that this represented more than ten millions in actual cash delivered, and all monies collected and paid beyond that were not the stealing necessarily of South Carolinians,

[20] 42nd Congress, 2nd Session, House Reports, II, No. 22, Part I, p. 120.

white or black, but the financial graft of Wall Street and its agents, made possible by the slander and reaction of the planters.

The rise of a group of a people is not a simultaneous shift of the whole mass; it is a continuous differentiation of individuals with inner strife and differences of opinion, so that individuals, groups and classes begin to appear seeking higher levels, groping for better ways, uniting with other like-minded bodies and movements. Every indication of this was present among Negroes during Reconstruction times. There was not a single reform movement, a single step toward protest, a single experiment for betterment in which Negroes were not found in varying numbers. The protest against corruption and inefficiency in South Carolina had in every case Negro adherents and in many cases Negro leaders.

The responsibility of Negroes for the government of South Carolina in Reconstruction was necessarily limited. They helped choose the elected officials and furnished a large number of the members of the legislature. But most of the administrative power was in the hands of the whites, and these were either Northerners, who had come South as officers or officials or to invest money, or native Southerners, both aristocrats and poor whites, who had undertaken to guide the Negro vote.

Francis B. Simkins:

NEW VIEWPOINTS OF SOUTHERN RECONSTRUCTION

THE issues of most periods of American history have been so satisfactorily settled that they are now significant only as possible explanations of aspects of contemporary events and institutions. This is not true of the main issue of the Reconstruction period: the great American race question. It is almost as timely today as when it arose in 1865; as one of its prominent students says, like Banquo's ghost it will not down. Consequently, interpretations of the ten or twelve years following the Civil War seem destined, for an indefinite period, to have an influence beyond mere explanations of past events. The successful historian of Reconstruction, by revealing early phases of the still burning race question, arouses more attention among the reading public than is usually accorded historical works.

This continued survival of the leading issue of the post-bellum era explains why the interpretations of those years are so varied and numerous. Conservative scholars have described the follies and rascalities of Negro politicians and their Carpetbagger friends so as to make the reader thankful that such knavery cannot be repeated in his time. Less scrupulous writers have so effectively correlated the events of Reconstruction with those of their own times that their books have been best sellers. The outstanding example of this is Claude Bowers' *Tragic Era*, in which an attack upon the Republican enemies of Alfred E. Smith in 1928 is veiled behind attacks upon the Republican leaders of 1868, 1872, and 1876. At least one novelist has so effectively connected certain lurid aspects of Reconstruction with the race prejudices prevailing in the South in his times that the situations he described have become a part of the Southern folk beliefs. The Ku Klux Klan is used as either a glamorous or sinister symbol for the arousal of issues of race, religion, and patriotism in which all Americans, radicals and reactionaries, Negro lovers and Negro haters, are vitally and perennially concerned. Reconstruction does not escape the attention of contemporary religionists; and even the Marxians, who would settle great social and economic issues, use Reconstruction experiences in their arguments.

A biased interpretation of Reconstruction caused one of the most important political developments in the recent history of the South, the disfranchisement of the blacks. The fraud and violence by which this objective was first obtained was justified on a single ground: the memory of the alleged horrors of Reconstruction. Later, amid a flood of oratory concerned with this memory, the white rulers of the South, in constitutional con-

Francis B. Simkins, "New Viewpoints of Southern Reconstruction," *Journal of Southern History*, V (February, 1939), 49–61. Used by permission.

ventions of the 1890's and 1900's, devised legal means to eliminate the Negro vote. "Reconstruction," asserted the prime justifier of this act, "was this villainy, anarchy, misrule and robbery, and I cannot, in any words that I possess, paint it." These words of Ben Tillman were endorsed by all shades of white opinion from Carter Glass, Henry W. Grady, and Charles B. Aycock to Tom Watson, Hoke Smith, and James K. Vardaman.

Historians, sensing that the discrediting of the period in which the Negro most freely participated in politics justifies his subsequent exclusion from those activities, have condemned the Reconstruction measures as sweepingly as have the Southern politicians. They have called the military rule by which these measures were inaugurated "as brutish a tyranny as ever marked the course of any government whose agents and organs claimed to be civilized"; they have termed the best of the Carpetbaggers "infamous scoundrels"; and they have described the enfranchised freedmen as belonging to a race "incapable of forming any judgment upon the actions of men." The article on South Carolina in the eleventh edition of the *Encyclopedia Britannica* in all seriousness concludes: "All the misfortunes of war itself are insignificant when compared with the sufferings of the people during Reconstruction."

The masses of white Southerners accept these judgments as axiomatic. White Southerners will argue the issues of the Civil War and even the merits of the Democratic party, but there is scarcely one in a position of authority who will debate Negro suffrage and the related issues of Reconstruction. The wickedness of this régime and the righteousness of the manner in which it was destroyed are fundamentals of his civic code. Such a condemnation or commendation justifies

the settlement of questions of the immediate past and are invoked to settle issues of even the remote future.

This extremely partisan judgment of still timely historical events imposes upon the historian of Reconstruction a serious civic duty. He must foster more moderate, saner, perhaps newer views of his period. This the present writer attempts to do in the light of his investigations of the processes of Reconstruction in the state where they were applied most radically.

The capital blunder of the chronicler of Reconstruction is to treat that period like Carlyle's portrayal of the French Revolution, as a melodrama involving wild-eyed conspirators whose acts are best described in red flashes upon a canvas. Such a treatment creates the impression that Southern society was frenzied by misery. This is at best the picturesque pageantry of the artist; at worst, the cheap sensationalism of the journalist or the scenario writer. At all odds it is woefully one-sided and unhistorical. Of course the South during Reconstruction, like France during the Revolution, had its prophets of despair, its fanatical idealists, its unprincipled knaves. Luckily the behavior of these damned souls is not the whole story of Reconstruction, but merely a partial recording of the political aspects of the era. Some of the political acts were as sane and constructive as those of the French Revolution. They were concerned with educational, constitutional, and political reform, and were instrumental in putting the Southern states in line with the progressive spirit of the nineteenth century.

The aberrations of the Reconstruction politicians were not accurate barometers of the actual behavior of the Southern people. The Reconstruction governments were not natural developments from the conditions inherent in Southern life, but were, in a sense, artificial impositions from without. Frenzied politics did not necessarily reflect a frenzied social life. Despite strange doings in statehouses, the Southern people of both races lived as quietly and as normally during Reconstruction as in any politically disturbed period before or after. The defiance of the traditional caste division occasionally expressed in an official reception or in an act of the legislature was not reflected generally in common social relations. No attempt was made to destroy white supremacy in the social or economic sphere or to sanction interracial marriages. The political aggressiveness of the Negroes, characteristic of the period, did not extend to other phases of human relations. A staunch Republican voter was often a good servant in the house of a white Democrat. Negro officeholders who were aggressive politically were known to observe carefully the etiquette of the Southern caste system.

Moreover, in aspects of life not directly political there were achievements during the post-bellum era so quietly constructive that they have escaped the attention of most historians. This is true even of DuBois, the colored author who ardently and extensively defends the Reconstruction record of his race.

Foremost among these achievements were agricultural reforms. While official agencies through Black Codes and the Freedmen's Bureau were making fragmentary and generally unsuccessful attempts to redefine a shattered rural economy, the freedmen bargained themselves into an agricultural situation unlike that of slavery and from their viewpoint advantageous. They worked beyond official purview. Although they were unable to gain legal title to the lands, they forced white competitors, for their labor in the expanding cotton fields, to establish them on separate farms in houses scattered over the land. This abandonment of the communal character of the Southern plantation bestowed upon the Negroes the American farmer's ideal of independent existence. This was a revolutionary reform more important in the actual life of the freedmen than the sensational but largely unsuccessful political changes attempted at the time. There followed the negotiation of share crop arrangements and other types of labor contracts between the freedmen and the landlords. These agreements soon became fixed by custom. They proved to be a satisfactory *modus vivendi* and demonstrated the possibility of the two races living together in harmony under a regimen of freedom.

Changes scarcely less significant took place in the religious sphere. Under slavery autonomous Negro churches had not been tolerated and blacks were forced to attend churches directed both administratively and doctrinally by the master race. During Reconstruction the freedmen successfully asserted religious freedom and established independent churches. This secession was accomplished with a minimum of ill feeling and without important doctrinal or ritualistic innovations by the seceding groups. But it was a momentous change in social relations. It has been permanent, having never been challenged by even the most reactionary social forces. Its importance to a people so intensely religious as are Southerners of both races is obvious. The existence of perfectly independent Negro churches has given the black race opportunity for self-expression studiously denied it since Reconstruction in political and other nonreligious fields.

Another radical but constructive change of a nonpolitical character was the development of a new commercial system. The breakup of the plantations into small units created much small trade and a consequent demand for small credit. This was met by the creation of the crossroads stores and the commercial villages and towns with stores and banks. These new institutions were owned by an emergent economic group, the storekeepers, who dominated the Southern community as effectively, if not as glamorously, as the planters had once done. The storekeepers were often also bankers, planters, church deacons, and sometimes state senators. Their power was based on large profits realized from the new system of credit advances on unharvested crops.

The assertion that the abnormalities of post-bellum politics did not adequately reflect the actualities of Southern life leads to the conviction that a balanced understanding of the period cannot be had without descriptions of social life. The social activities of both races remained relatively wholesome and happy; there was little of the misery, hatred, and repression often sweepingly ascribed to it by writers. There were camp meetings, dances, balls, tournaments, picnics, parades, agricultural fairs, lavish banquets, and indulgence in the vanities of personal adornment. There was, of course, much poverty, the shadow of the Lost Cause, and apprehension concerning possible events in the political world. But there were fresh memories of heroic events, and there were surviving warriors to give glamorous reality to these memories. Gaiety was disciplined by recent tragedy, but it was not dampened by the utilitarianism of a more progressive age.

The claim that the times were completely dominated by stark pessimism is refuted by the fact that during Reconstruction the optimistic concept called the New South was born. It is true that predictions concerning a new civilization springing from the ruins of slavery and the Confederacy were premature. It was ridiculous to call newspapers established amid the ruins of Columbia and the rice plantations *The Phoenix* and *The New South*. But the spirit of progress abroad in the land was not stifled by varied difficulties. It was fostered by some hopeful actualities — a new commercial life, the new banks, the high price of cotton, and the new agriculture made possible by the first extensive use of commercial fertilizer. An optimistic note was reflected in the newspapers. When in the 1880's this hopefulness germinated in the actualities of new industries and a philosophy of progress and reconciliation, it was from the seeds sown in the two previous decades.

In one sense, those who have essayed books on Reconstruction have closed their narratives before the actual reconstruction of the South began. The Northern reformers who arrived in the 1860's and 1870's carrying carpetbags were driven out by Southerners armed with shotguns before these outsiders could make their projects effective. But a later generation of Northern reformers, coming mostly in the twentieth century, have experienced a different reception. Riding in expensive automobiles, emanating an aura of wealth, this later generation have, through lavish expenditures, received the enthusiastic co-operation of Southerners. They have introduced Northern ideals of literature, architecture, and landscaping, and have instilled into the Southern mind a definite preference for Northern concepts of civilization.

Those of us who are not willing to accept this thesis that the true reconstruction did not come until years after the so-called Reconstruction, should nevertheless feel obligated to watch for evidence during the 1870's of the beginnings of the industrial, cultural, and psychical conquest by the North of the South which has shown itself so clearly in recent decades. Perhaps hidden beneath the seemingly premature and erratic actions of the Carpetbaggers were plans which have been executed by the rich Northerners of the twentieth century.

As has been suggested, one of the most striking features of Southern society is the color line. This division under slavery was not as sharp as it is today. The influences of Reconstruction induced this sharpening. The aggressiveness of the blacks and their allies caused resentment among the whites and consequent estrangement between the races. This alienation in turn caused the blacks, especially in social and economic relations, to grow more independent. If this thesis is true, the careful student of the post-bellum period is obligated to isolate those interests and attitudes which account for the intensification of the caste division of Southern society. In doing this he will perhaps help explain the most important reality of interracial relations.

One of the accepted conventions of Reconstruction scholars is that the Carpetbaggers failed because their measures were excessively radical. We have often been told how the Four Million were suddenly hurled from slavery into freedom; how black barbarians were forced to attempt the roles of New England gentlemen; how seven hundred thousand of these illiterates were given the vote and the privilege of office-holding. But were these measures genuine radicalism, actual uprootings which inevitably led to fundamental changes in Southern society? The answer is that they were scarcely more than artificial or superimposed remedies from the outside which

in no real sense struck at the roots of Southern life.

A truly radical program would have called for the confiscation of land for the freedmen. Land was the principal form of Southern wealth, the only effective weapon with which the ex-slaves could have battled for economic competence and social equality. But the efforts of the Freedmen's Bureau in the direction of land endowments for its wards were fitful and abortive. Conservative constitutional theory opposed any such meaningful enfranchisement. The dominant Radicalism of the day naively assumed that a people's salvation could be obtained through the ballot and the spelling book. The freedmen got these but were allowed to continue in physical want, and even lost the industrial skills and disciplines they had inherited from slavery. No wonder they carried bags in which to bear away their suffrage and expected education to place them at the tables of the rich and competent. They were realists and their so-called benefactors were the deluded ones. Wise Tory statesmen like Bismarck, Lord Salisbury, and Alexander II would have put something in their bags and endowed them with tangible social privilege.

In another vital respect the so-called Radicals of the 1860's lost an opportunity to attempt genuine radicalism. They did not try to destroy the greatest obstacle to the Negroes' salvation, the Southern caste system. Contemporary professions of such attempts lack sincerity. Anglo-Saxon race pride, New England standards of civilization, a respect for narrowly Protestant standards of morality were in the way. Attempts at fraternization between the races were stilted official affairs lacking in that unconscious informality on which true sociability must be based. No one was ever allowed to forget that race distinctions existed.

A distinguished Negro lecturer recently stated that the whole truth is not told by those books which assert that the blacks and their coadjutors were the sole aggressors of the Reconstruction period. Revolution was attempted on both sides. The blacks, of course, on their part, were sufficiently aggressive to demand the continuation of freedom and the vote and the liberties implied in these terms. But the whites also showed an aggressiveness which went beyond the maintenance of their traditional position in Southern society. They tightened the bonds of caste; they deprived the subordinate caste of many occupational opportunities enjoyed under slavery; they drove colored farmers from the land; they gradually deprived the blacks of a well-integrated position and imposed on them a status akin to pariahs whom many wished exiled. The disappearance of aristocratic prejudices against many forms of honest labor created the conviction that it was possible for Southern society to function without the despised African. Certainly an appraisal of the helplessness of the blacks at the close of the Reconstruction era makes one wonder why the whites are not more often adjudged the actual revolutionaries of the times. Victory was in white hands — the actuality as well as the sentiment and the tradition.

Several generations of historians have asserted that the Reconstruction governments were so grievously corrupt and extravagant that they checked all efforts at material rehabilitation. There was, of course, corruption and waste — expensive spittoons, thousand dollar bribes, fraudulent bonds, and so on. But the actual financial burdens of government which tolerated such acts have been exagger-

ated. Their expenditures seem small when compared with the budgets of twentieth-century states and extravagant only against the parsimony of the governments immediately preceding and following. The extravagant bond issues of the Reconstruction governments were not an immediate burden upon contemporaries and afflicted subsequent generations only to the extent to which they were not repudiated. The Radical governments, like the government of Louis XVI in France, failed not because their expenditures were burdensome but because they did not enjoy enough power and respect to force the taxpayers to yield funds sufficient to discharge the obligations of effective political establishments. There was a taxpayers' strike rather than a tax collectors' orgy. Some Reconstruction governments could not pay their gas bills.

A reinterpretation of the tax policies of the Radical régimes suggests a new explanation of the odius reputations possessed by these governments. Of course, a partial answer is that there was corruption and incompetence. Illiterate freedmen were easily seduced by unscrupulous Carpetbaggers and Scalawags. But were these malpractices the most serious offenses of the Reconstructionists? It seems that the worst crime of which they have been adjudged guilty was the violation of the American caste system. The crime of crimes was to encourage Negroes in voting, officeholding, and other functions of social equality. This supposedly criminal encouragement of the Negro is execrated ever more savagely as with the passing years race prejudices continue to mount. Mild-mannered historians declare that the assertiveness resulting therefrom was grotesque and abnormal, while the more vehement writers call it the worst of civic scandals. Attempts to make the Reconstruction governments reputable and honest have been treated with scorn, and the efforts of Negroes to approach the white man's standards of civilization are adjudged more reprehensible than the behavior of the more ignorant and corrupt. Social equality and negroism have not a chance to be respectable.

Such views logically grow out of the conviction that the Negro belongs to an innately inferior race and is therefore incapable by his very nature of exercising with sagacity the higher attributes of civilization. James Ford Rhodes gives the viewpoint of moderate historians by declaring the Negro to be "one of the most inferior races of mankind" and by endorsing Brinton's theory of the Negro's arrested development at adolescence. John W. Burgess voices the opinions of the more prejudiced when he says: "The claim that there is nothing in the color of the skin is a great sophism. A black skin means membership in a race of men which has never succeeded in subjecting passion to reason." Less critical writers take such statements as so obviously true that they need no specific affirmation.

The impartial historian, however, cannot so readily endorse this finding. His knowledge of the conclusions of modern anthropology casts grave doubts on the innate inferiority of the blacks. This knowledge, indeed, creates the necessity of explaining the conduct of the Negroes, during Reconstruction as well as during other times, on other than racial grounds. It also leads to the rejection of the gloomy generalization that the race, because of its inherent nature, is destined to play forever its present inferior role. Loose assertions concerning Reconstruction as an attempt to return to the ideals of the jungle, as an effort to re-

barbarize the Negro and to make South Carolina and Mississippi into African provinces, seem to have no basis in truth. Indeed, the exact opposite seems nearer the truth. Reconstruction can be interpreted as a definite step forward in the Anglicization or the Americanization of the blacks, certainly not their Africanization. The sagacious William A. Dunning tells the truth when he asserts that the newly-liberated freedmen were "fascinated with the pursuit of the white man's culture." This passion did not abate during the later years of Reconstruction; it is still a dominant feature of Negro life. The zeal with which the ex-slaves sought the benefits of literary education is unparalleled in history; this was the most obvious means of assimilating the white man's culture. Although Negro society during the first years of freedom tended to grow independent of white society, it continued to imitate the culture of the superior caste. Among the more cultivated Negroes, the more independent their society is of the whites, the stronger the resemblance. The radical changes in Negro religion which grew out of freedom were not in the direction of Africa, but rather in the direction of frontier or backwoods America, with some imitations of Fifth Avenue standards of clerical correctness. The misbehavior of Negro politicians had no African coloring. Their bad manners were those of American rustics and their vices were not unlike those of contemporary Tammany politicians. It is true that variations in the dialect of the Southern Negroes were most pronounced in the years after the war, or at least they were then best recognized; but even in the Gullah speech of the Sea Islands, African words did not predominate.

The efforts of certain Negroes of the post-bellum period to establish African connections were abortive. When cultured Negroes of the type of Martin R. Dulany tried to discover their African ancestors, they were guilty of a fatuous Americanism, different only in one respect from that of those Americans who trace their ancestors in England: the African quest could not be successful. The influences of slavery had resulted in such a thorough Americanization of the blacks that little African was left in their culture. This was the main reason why the efforts during Reconstruction to promote emigration to Liberia were a dismal failure. There was no more cultural affinity between the Southern Negro and his African blood kin than between the American Negro and the Chinese.

The aspersions on the freedmen for emulating the white man's culture have been as unfair as the criticisms of them for the alleged attempt to Africanize the South. Numerous writers have ridiculed sooty women for wearing veils and gloves, for carrying umbrellas, for calling themselves "Mrs." and "Miss," and for retiring from the fields to establish firesides and homes. Likewise, the spectacle of Negro politicians trying to talk like Daniel Webster or Charles Sumner has caused jest, and undue emphasis has been placed upon the impracticability of the attempt to load the curricula of Negro schools with items of classical culture adapted from New England. But are these criticisms just? It is granted that such aspirations after the white man's culture were often the result of uncritical enthusiasms and were beyond the immediate reach of an inexperienced people turned loose naked in the world. But measured according to the unescapable standards of American civilization, were these aspirations in the wrong direction? Were they not in the direction all Americans, including even those relegated to the lowest caste, seek to travel? The major problem of the American Negro is to attain the standards of American civilization. This is a decree of circumstances which the American Negro has accepted without reluctance. Therefore, the Reconstructionists who held Boston and Massachusetts up as ideals for the blacks were not giving the wrong advice. The fact that this advice moved the Negroes profoundly, if not always sagaciously, is a tribute to the sound instincts of these blacks and of their Reconstruction mentors.

Historians of the South should adopt a more critical, creative, and tolerant attitude toward so important a period in the annals of their section as Reconstruction. This will promote truth and scholarship in the austere sense of those terms. It will do more. It will banish that provincialism which is based on priggishness and ignorance of comparisons; it will fortify the sound provincialism born of better understanding of one's own province; and it will enrich those measured evaluations which are possible only after contact with other people's provinces. A better comprehension of the Reconstruction past will aid in the solution of the South's great race problem. Bias and passion should be explained in rational terms in order that contemporaries may better understand the forces motivating them. In this modest way the great civic obligation of the historian can be discharged.

E. Merton Coulter:

BLACKOUT OF HONEST GOVERNMENT

> As each generation feels constrained to rewrite the past, points of view and methods of approach necessarily change, and so revisionists arise. If they remain within the reasonable bounds of established facts, they may well make lasting contributions in fresher interpretations and in the presentation of new information; but if they depart from the old channels to attract attention in novel and unsubstantiated points of view, they themselves may soon be revised. The author of this work feels that there can be no sensible departure from the well-known facts of the Reconstruction program as it was applied to the South. No amount of revision can write away the grievous mistakes made in this abnormal period of American history. This writer, therefore, has not attempted it. [Preface, p. xi. Italics supplied by editor.]

CONGRESS had set up new state governments because, as it claimed, the Johnson states were illegal and did not protect life and property. New leaders under new constitutions now took charge; the elimination of the old Southern leaders, from top to bottom, had been the heart of the Congressional plan. Would Congressional governments succeed better than Johnson governments — or even nearly as well?

Intent upon filling the thousands of offices made vacant, the delegates of the constitutional conventions maneuvered themselves into the best ones, and set up machinery which controlled the rest. In some of the states a few Conservatives slipped into minor offices. Governors were empowered to fill most of the local offices by appointment; legislatures could declare offices vacant and provide for filling them to their liking; and returning

boards, a new Radical device for counting ballots, could manipulate the votes to bring about any desired result. In addition to the state offices, there were Federal positions to be filled, both elective and appointive — Congressmen, judges, customs collectors, revenue agents, and postmasters. As noted, all elective offices the Radicals controlled and all appointive offices fell into their hands when President Johnson gave way to Grant in 1869. Now all Southern officialdom became a powerful Radical machine. Even Federal judges became miserably partisan and corrupt. John C. Underwood in Virginia thoroughly disgraced himself in the proceedings relative to the trial of Jefferson Davis and by his political manipulations; Richard Busteed in Alabama debauched his bench through a rich harvest of bribes in cases brought before him by collusion; and Edward H. Durell in Louisiana be-

E. Merton Coulter, *The South during Reconstruction, 1865–1877* (Vol. VIII of *A History of the South*, ed. by Wendell Holmes Stephenson and E. Merton Coulter, Baton Rouge: Louisiana State University Press and The Littlefield Fund for Southern History of the University of Texas, 1947), pp. xi, 139–161.

came so completely a part of the corruption in that state that he resigned to escape impeachment.[1]

Most of the people who filled the many offices were untrained and untried — Scalawags, Carpetbaggers, and Negroes. Had the times been normal their duties would have been onerous and complicated; with the times out of joint they took the easy road and speedily buried themselves in corruption. Carpetbaggers filled a majority of the higher offices. In the first elections in the seven states admitted in 1868, four of the governors, ten of the fourteen United States Senators, and twenty of the thirty-five Representatives were Carpetbaggers. Throughout the whole period of Reconstruction nineteen Carpetbaggers went to the Senate. Some of the outstanding ones who held high offices were: in South Carolina, Daniel H. Chamberlain, native of Massachusetts and educated at Harvard and Yale colleges, mostly honest, but succumbing ultimately to party necessities, and B. Frank Wittemore, also from Massachusetts, thoroughly corrupt, and expelled from Congress; in Mississippi, Adelbert Ames, son-in-law of Benjamin F. Butler, resigning the army to enter politics, crusading and inept, fleeing the governorship to escape impeachment; in

Louisiana, Henry Clay Warmoth of Illinois, entering the political scene poor and retiring rich, and William Pitt Kellogg, born in Vermont and growing up in Illinois, leading his adopted state government into a blackout of honesty; and in Arkansas, Powell Clayton, passing from a disgraced governorship to the United States Senate.[2]

Although the Carpetbaggers played an important part in every state, they were not uniformly strong. In Virginia, North Carolina, Georgia, Tennessee, and Texas, the Scalawags came to be dominant, and, therefore, all that was reprehensible in Radical rule in the South should not be placed on Northern importation. The pestilences of the times knew no limits either geographical or racial; native-born white Southerners became as corrupt as Carpetbaggers, and only in South Carolina and Louisiana did the Negroes ever have a majority in any legislature.

And yet the most spectacular and exotic development in government in the history of white civilization was to be seen in the part the Negroes played in ruling the South — longest to be remembered, shuddered at, and execrated. An English traveler could hardly believe his senses as he saw the Negroes made "King, Lords, and Commons, and something more," and in South Carolina he observed "a proletariat Parliament . . . the like of which could not be produced

---

[1] These judges had been appointed before the Radicals took charge of the South. Avary, *Dixie after the War*, 237–44; Fleming, *Civil War and Reconstruction in Alabama*, 744; John W. Burgess, *Reconstruction and the Constitution, 1866–1876* (New York, 1902), 270–71. Nordhoff, *Cotton States*, 85, said the Alabama election law set up "one of the most perfect machines for political fraud that I have ever heard of." In Plaquemines Parish, Louisiana, one name out of every seven and one-half people in the white population was put on the registration books, but one name out of every three and one-eighth of the colored people received a place on the list. Many of the names were, of course, fictitious; out of forty-eight names drawn on a jury, thirty-six were nonexistent. *Ibid.*, 66.

[2] Dunning, *Reconstruction*, 120; Reginald C. McGrane, *Foreign Bondholders and American State Debts* (New York, 1935), 313; C. Mildred Thompson, "Carpet-Baggers in the United States Senate," in *Studies in Southern History and Politics*, 161–66. Warmoth, whose salary as governor was $8,000 a year, admitted making over $100,000 his first year in office. By 1872 his wealth was estimated at $500,000 to $1,000,000. Fleming (ed.), *Documentary History of Reconstruction*, II, 39. So outraged did some communities feel that they refused to let officials take their seats. Stearns, *Black Man of the South*, 212–40.

under the widest suffrage in any part of the world save in some of these Southern States." As a Southerner saw the South's predicament, "What a white commune was in France we all have seen; what a negro commune is in America our eyes have also witnessed. Both made war on intelligence and social distinctions, both brought chaos in their train."[3]

Though the Northern Radicals instituted Negro suffrage and officeholding in the name of justice, they were thoroughly insincere in their protestations; for in the first place few of the Northern states allowed the Negroes to vote and none ever promoted a Negro into any office, however intelligent the Negro or however lowly the position. Furthermore, the Radical national government, unrestrained by state laws or suffrage requirements, waited long to appoint Negroes to office in the North. Seeing these inconsistencies, a delegation of Negroes, representing both North and South, begged President Grant in 1869 to select some Northern Negroes.[4] A Southerner prayed that "some Boston Sambo may be appointed postmaster in that city so that the Puritans of that place may get a dose of the physic they have prepared for the South."[5] Why had no Negro been elected to office in the North? "Why has such a negro, for example, as Frederick Douglass," asked a Southerner, "never been sent by the Radicals of New York to represent his city of Rochester in the Legislature of the State or in the Congress of the nation?"[6] Until a Negro should sit in Congress, representing a Northern state, "and a score of colored men shall sit in the Legislature of each of the New England States, then, and not till then," said a Missourian, "will the black man be as well treated in those Radical regions, as he is now treated in the rebel States of the South."[7]

Carpetbaggers were as little desirous of promoting Negroes into high office in the South as their Northern colleagues were in their states; and Scalawags, actuated by racial antipathies more than Carpetbaggers, objected to Negroes holding any offices. Both were quite desirous that Negroes vote — but not for Negroes. A Georgia Negro wrote Charles Sumner that there was no other place in the Union where there were so "many miserable hungry unscrupulous politicians . . . and if they could prevent it no colored man would ever occupy any office of profit or trust." He later wrote, "I am tired of being used as stepping-stones to elevate white men alone to office and would like to vote for some competent colored man" to go to the United States Senate.[8] A convention of Negroes in Macon resolved in 1868 that they did not recommend the colored man "to be satisfied with being a mere pack horse, to ride white men into office, whether he [sic] is the exponent of our sentiments or not; no, it would be better that we did not have the Ballot."[9] Even so, Negroes frequently held offices far beyond their capacity to administer them.

In South Carolina, Florida, Mississippi, and Louisiana the Negroes reached the zenith of their power, but in no state was a Negro ever elected to the governorship,

[3] Somers, *Southern States since the War*, 41; *Southern Magazine*, XIV (1874), 587.

[4] Montgomery *Alabama State Journal*, May 22, 1869.

[5] Dalton *North Georgia Citizen*, May 27, 1869.

[6] Augusta *Weekly Chronicle & Sentinel*, September 16, 1874.

[7] *Missouri Republican*, quoted *ibid.*, June 8, 1870.

[8] Belcher, Augusta, Ga., to Sumner, April 5, 1869, in Sumner Papers, Box 94, No. 9; Belcher to Sumner, February 3, 1870, *ibid.*, Box 96, No. 99.

[9] Macon *American Union*, October 9, 1868.

though in South Carolina, Mississippi, and Louisiana Negroes became lieutenant governors. In Mississippi the lieutenant governor, Alexander K. Davis, frequently acted as governor during the absence of Ames; and in Louisiana, Lieutenant Governor Pinchback succeeded to the governorship if it be admitted that in the jigsaw puzzle of politics in that state Governor Warmoth was legally impeached and removed. All other state offices in some state at one time or another were filled by Negroes — but in only one state was a justice of the Supreme Court a Negro. South Carolina elevated to this position Jonathan Jasper Wright, a colored Carpetbagger from Pennsylvania.[10] The great majority of Negro officeholders were local officials — such as constables, justices of the peace, county superintendents of education, etc. — though in all the states there was a sprinkling of Negroes in the legislatures, ranging in number from only one in Tennessee to a majority in some of the sessions of the South Carolina legislature. It was a bitter comment among Negroes that Brownlow, the most Radical of native Southerners, saw to it that few of their race attained office in Tennessee.

White members of most state legislatures disliked the presence of Negroes; in Georgia in 1868 resentment gained the ascendancy and the white members, Radicals and Conservatives, banded together and expelled them. In later sessions when they reappeared at the behest of Congress and the army, the editor of the legislative manual merely recorded their names without the customary biographical sketches, explaining that there was nothing to say about them beyond

their having been waiters, bootblacks, and cotton-field hands. He slyly admitted another motive: "though Congress could compel him to associate with negroes in a deliberative body, sit beside them in railroad cars, etc., neither Congress, Military Government, a triple reconstruction nor even another amendment to the national patch-work, the United States Constitution, could compel him to publish their biographies in this book."[11]

A considerable number of Negroes were appointed to Federal positions in the South, such as postmasters and mail agents, but the highest Federal service performed by Negroes was in Congress. Southerners looked with some degree of complacency on Negroes going to Congress, for there Northerners would see Negro rulers in operation and would be forced to associate with them. Since Negroes would not make corn, or cotton, or sugar, it might be that they would make laws. "We want negroes to be so thick in Congress," said a Virginian, "that a man standing on the wharf at Aquia Creek, with a favorable wind, could smell them. We want their wool to be knee-deep in the halls of Congress, and we do not want any one there who is not five times blacker than the ace of spades."[12]

In the summer of 1868 a South Carolina Radical inquired of Charles Sumner whether he thought it would "injure the republican party in the North and West if [we] were to send some colored men to Congress."[13] It was apparently not considered bad politics, for during the next dozen years seven Southern states

---

[10] Robert H. Woody, "Jonathan Jasper Wright, Associate Justice of the Supreme Court of South Carolina, 1870–77," in *Journal of Negro History*, XVIII (1933), 114–31.

[11] Alexander St. Clair-Abrams, *Manual and Biographical Register of the State of Georgia for 1871–2* (Atlanta, 1872), vi.

[12] Richmond *Times*, quoted in *Southern Cultivator*, XXIV (1866), 61.

[13] W. B. Nash, Columbia, S. C., to Sumner, August 22, 1868, in Sumner Papers, Box 87, No. 18.

sent as Senators and Representatives twenty-eight Negroes. The greatest number at any one time was eight in 1875. The states sending Negroes were North Carolina, South Carolina, Georgia, Florida, Alabama, Mississippi, and Louisiana. Mississippi sent the first one in the person of Hiram R. Revels, as Senator, born a free Negro in North Carolina. Only two Negro Senators ever served in Congress, both from Mississippi. Pinchback, the Louisiana mulatto, succeeded in getting himself elected both to the House and Senate for overlapping terms, but he was not seated in either place. Some of these Negro Congressmen did creditable service, but others became either echoes of their Radical masters or disgusting troublemakers. Their service did not recommend their race to the South or even to the North, for not until the twentieth century did a Negro sit in Congress from any Northern state.[14]

It would have been remarkable had Negroes shown any conspicuous ability as lawmakers and rulers, though they were better than there was reason to expect; but even so, much of their performance was either grotesque or puerile. Psychologically and in every other respect the Negroes were fearfully unprepared to occupy positions of rulership. Race and color came to mean more to them than any other consideration, whether of honest government, of justice to the individual, or even of ultimate protection of their own rights. Negroes on juries let color blind them, and they rejected the wisest counsel, Northern and Southern, against banding together politically, instead of dividing on issues

and policies of government. Of course, many white Conservatives made it difficult for them to do otherwise; but Negroes proscribed their own race if any voted Democratic — their preachers excommunicating them, their womenfolk bringing all their feminine powers to play against them, and Loyal Leagues intimidating and doing violence to them.[15] Their idea of the new order was

> De bottom rail's on de top,
> An' we's gwine to keep it dar.[16]

Radical leaders impressed their views on the Negroes. An Alabama editor said, "The Radicals are now trying to persuade the Southern negroes that it was very cruel and inhuman to rescue them from the dinner pot — that it would have been much better for them had their forefathers been eaten in Africa. Perhaps it would. If they intend to let carpetbaggers and scallawags lead them by their noses forever we are sure it would have been. Any man had better be eaten than a 'born fool' forever or the father of a generation of fools."[17]

Most Negro officeholders were more to be pitied than blamed, but a few blatant, dishonest, insolent megalomaniacs

14 Samuel D. Smith, The Negro in Congress, 1870–1901 (Chapel Hill, 1940), 3–9, 45, 137–44; William A. Russ, Jr., "The Negro and White Disfranchisement during Radical Reconstruction," in Journal of Negro History, XIX (1934), 171–92.

15 As an example of a sensible attitude, a Negro candidate wrote, "I am for peace and harmony, and utterly opposed to any discussions having a tendency to excite bad feeling between any classes of society; and in canvassing the District I shall so conduct myself as to merit that respect and kindness which has always been shown me." Greenville Southern Enterprise, April 1, 1868.

16 King, Great South, 453.

17 Montgomery Weekly Advertiser, August 18, 1875. This is part of a Radical hand-bill to impress Negroes: "Every man knows that the Republican Party, under the lead of God, President Lincoln and General Grant, freed the whole colored race from slavery; and every man who knows anything, believes that the Democratic party will, if they can, make them slaves again." Dalton North Georgia Citizen, September 10, 1868.

discredited all. A Carpetbagger characterized Henry M. Turner, preacher, politician, and presider at many Negro conventions, as "a licentious robber and counterfeiter, a vulgar blackguard, a sacrilegious profaner of God's name, and a most consummate hypocrite." Yet the Negroes elected him to the Georgia legislature —"if he had received his deserts, he would have gone to the Penitentiary"; he was "a thief and a scoundrel, and yet they voted for him." "If the colored people have not the elements of morality among them sufficiently to cry down such shameless characters, they should not expect to command the respect of decent people anywhere."[18] One Southerner told Sumner that he treated Negroes kindly, "but to Sit still and allow an ignoramus to represent me in government Councils I am not a going to do it & you know that no senseble [sic] man will."[19] Another, seeing the humorous side of a Negro candidate, said, "Ike has no 'book larnin,' but he bakes an excellent wheat pone, and knows how to drive a hack."[20]

General William S. Rosecrans, amidst a Confederate atmosphere at White Sulphur Springs, asked General Lee, in writing, whether he thought the South must in reality be ruled by "the poor, simple, uneducated, landless freedmen" under the corrupt leadership of whites still worse. Lee and thirty-one other prominent Southerners signed an answer declaring their opposition, basing it on no enmity toward freedmen, "but from a deep-seated conviction that at present the negroes have neither the intelligence nor other qualifications which are neces-

sary to make them depositories of political power."[21] The minority report of a Congressional committee declared, "History, till now, gives no account of a conqueror so cruel as to place his vanquished foes under the domination of their former slaves. *That was reserved for the radical rulers in this great Republic.*"[22]

South Carolina and Louisiana, apart from Haiti, were the world's classic examples of Negro rule, but worse than Haiti, for the black emperors of that benighted country ruled over black people who had never known any other kind of rule but bad. The general character of Negro government in these states was dismal and devastating in the extreme. It meant that the protection which civilized communities had received from their governments was at an end. Heretofore, if conditions should become too bad there was always an irreducible minimum of intelligence to which an outraged people could turn for redress; in these states that irreducible minimum miraculously had been reduced to nothing, for no appeal could be made to ignorant Negro majorities. One of the first questions put to a stranger coming to New Orleans to see the sights was whether he had seen the Negro legislature in action; and *Appletons' Hand-Book of American Travel* advised tourists that a peep into the statehouse in Columbia would "be intensely interesting and should not be missed by those who desire to see the negro in the role of a statesman."[23]

---

18 Macon *American Union*, December 29, 1870; June 15, 1871.

19 Unsigned letter, Ft. Gaines, Ga., to Sumner, October 5, 1868, in Sumner Papers, Box 87, No. 74.

20 Tallahassee *Sentinel*, September 2, 1867.

21 Augusta *Weekly Constitutionalist*, September 16, 1868.

22 *Ku Klux Conspiracy*, I, 438. "Now, we have as our rulers the vilest of mankind, whom no gentleman would allow to enter his kitchen," said the *Land We Love*, VI (1868–1869), 174.

23 Charles H. Jones (ed.), *Appletons' Hand-Book of American Travel, Southern Tour . . .* (New York, 1874), 132.

Specifically, the South Carolina House in 1873 consisted of 124 members, of whom 23 were Conservatives. Of the remaining 101 Radicals, 94 were Negroes. The Negroes thus outnumbered the whites more than three to one, though the Negro population of South Carolina was only slightly larger than the white. The Negro legislators were of all shades, from the lightest mulattoes to the blackest negroids, fresh from the kitchen and the field, in clothing ranging from secondhand black frock coats to the "coarse and dirty garments of the field." The white members did or said little, stunned by what they saw and heard — voluble, jabbering Negroes, always raising points of order and personal privilege, speaking a half dozen times on the same question, and repeating themselves constantly without knowing it. A South Carolinian viewed the scene for a time and as he turned away exclaimed, "My God, look at this! . . . Let me go." A Northern newspaperman who came down to see this amazing spectacle declared it was "barbarism overwhelming civilization by physical force" and "a wonder and a shame to modern civilization." A black parliament representing a white constituency — the only example in all history![24]

Saddled with an irresponsible officialdom, the South was now plunged into debauchery, corruption, and private plundering unbelievable — suggesting that government had been transformed into an engine of destruction. It was fortunate for the South that its officials were bent on private aggrandizement and personal gain, rather than on a fundamental class overturning which would have resulted in confiscations and an upset of civilization. This condition was, therefore, nothing more than the Southern side

24 Pike, *Prostrate State*, 10–16.

of the national picture. Corruption permeated government from the statehouse to the courthouse and city hall — though in local government there was a tendency for more honesty to assert itself under the closer scrutiny of the people. Yet it is probably true that New Orleans suffered as much from misgovernment as Chicago and Boston did from fire.

The variety of means used to debauch government and plunder the public treasury bespeaks the vivid imaginations and practical ability of the perpetrators. Every seceded state came under the withering hand of Radical rule, but it was reserved to South Carolina, Louisiana, and Arkansas to suffer most. Legislatures piled up expenses against their impoverished states to fantastic heights. In Florida the cost of printing in 1869 was more than the entire cost of the state government in 1860; and the legislature sold for five cents an acre 1,100,000 acres of public land held in trust. The Georgia legislature bought from a favored agent in Atlanta an unfinished opera house for $250,000, previously sold for much less, to convert it into a capitol building. In Arkansas a Negro was given $9,000 for repairing a bridge which had originally cost $500. Brownlow of Tennessee, too palsied to sign his name, gave wide authority to others to attach his signature to state bonds with results easily imagined. In South Carolina the legislature bought for $700,000 land worth $100,000 for resale to Negroes; it issued $1,590,000 worth of bonds with which to redeem $500,000 worth of bank notes, and paid $75,000 to take a state census in 1869, although the Federal census was due to be taken the following year, which cost only $43,000; it voted extra compensation of $1,000 to the speaker for his efficient service when he lost $1,000 on a horse race; it paid for lunches, whiskies and wines, women's apparel, and coffins charged by the legislators to legislative expenses; and Governor Scott while drunk was induced by a fancy lady in a burlesque show to sign an issue of state bonds. The Louisiana legislature was extremely ingenious in devising means of spending the state's money: Before the war its sessions had cost on an average of $100,000 but under Radical rule they cost about $1,000,000, half of which was for the mileage expenses and salaries of the members and clerks; its printing bill under three years of Warmoth's rule was $1,500,000 although previously it had never amounted to more than $60,000 for a year; to provide a capitol building it paid $250,000 for the St. Louis Hotel, recently sold for $84,000; it chartered the Mississippi Valley Navigation Company and purchased $100,000 worth of stock in it, though it never organized to do business; it chartered a Society to Prevent Cruelty to Animals, whose activities turned out to be rustling stray animals in New Orleans and holding them for $5.00 a day charges to the owners and arresting horses left standing in the streets while their riders were transacting business in the shops; and the chief justice was a party to the sale of a state-owned railroad for $50,000 on which had been expended more than $2,000,000, refusing to sell it at a higher price to bidders whom he did not favor. The cost of clerks and assistants amounted to as much as the total expenses of wartime sessions; legislatures created new offices and increased the salaries of the old ones and created new counties for the spoils that went with them; governors pardoned criminals for pecuniary and political reasons, and legislation was regularly bought and sold, one Louisiana legislator demanding the price of his vote though he had been absent — and so the

record of corruption could be extended *ad infinitum.*[25]

Whether or not the purpose of Radical Reconstruction was to place "the negro and the almighty dollar in the sanctionary of the Constitution,"[26] there was ample evidence in Southern state documents of the intention to do both. Yet these constitutions were considered then and since as proof of the desires of the framers to promote true democracy and economic recovery. Whatever the motives, the results were devastating to honest government, for they opened up to dishonest speculators, Northern and Southern, the exploitation of Southern credit in the name of railroad development. In these robberies stand high the names of George W. Swepson and Martin S. Littlefield in North Carolina and Florida, Hannibal I. Kimball in Georgia, and John C. and Daniel N. Stanton in Alabama. In every state there were individuals or groups that seized their opportunities.

The process was simple and appeared entirely divorced from corruption; in fact, it was nothing new, for it had been used in the South before the war and directly following, before the Radicals had secured control of the government. It consisted merely in the state lending its credit to private companies in their efforts to construct railroads, by buying their stock, by guaranteeing the payment of railroad bonds, and by giving

[25] *Ibid.*, 49, 191–97, 199, 213; Nordhoff, *Cotton States*, 31, 43, 47, 56, 59, 60, 62; Ella Lonn, *Reconstruction in Louisiana after 1868* (New York, 1918), 30, 34, 50, 87; Davis, *Civil War and Reconstruction in Florida*, 648–50, 666–67, 670–71; Robert H. Woody (ed.), "Behind the Scenes in the Reconstruction Legislature of South Carolina: Diary of Josephus Woodruff," in *Journal of Southern History*, II (1936), 78–102, 233–59; Simkins and Woody, *South Carolina during Reconstruction*, 113, 134–140; Coulter, *William G. Brownlow*, 376–77.

[26] Minority report, *Ku Klux Conspiracy*, I, 525.

them a fixed sum for each mile constructed, and in the last two methods
taking a mortgage on the railroad. A
Georgia Conservative said, "[It] is now
quite apparent that the public mind has,
with very considerable unanimity, accepted 'State aid' as the true policy of the
State,"[27] and an Alabama Radical agreed
that it was *"in no sense a party measure."*[28] It was only through the dishonesties of state officials that the great
stench in railroad aid arose. In violation
of law they delivered bonds before the
railroads were built, and the dishonest
promoters sold these bonds for what they
could get and never built the roads.
Sometimes legislatures also loaned more
per mile than the roads were worth when
finished, so that even with the roads
turned over to the states, considerable
losses were suffered. The amount usually
allowed was from $10,000 to $15,000 a
mile, to be paid as ten-mile units were
completed.   Counties also lent their
credit. A Chicago editor declared that
guarantees were claimed "and generally
obtained for anything which had two
parallel bars of iron, however light, upon
any apology for a road-bed," and, he
might have added, for nothing at all.[29]
Every state suffered under these dishonesties except Mississippi, where there
was a constitutional provision against
state aid, but the legislatures got around
it by making outright gifts to certain
favored companies.[30]

North   Carolina   authorized   almost
$28,000,000 of railroad bonds and actu-
ally delivered over $17,500,000; on ac-

count of ill-kept records, Alabama could
never determine the amount of her
issues, but it has been estimated from
$17,000,000 to $30,000,000; a ring of
twenty men controlled the charters of
eighty-six railroads in Arkansas and got
state loans to the amount of $5,350,000,
to which was added $3,000,000 in levee
bonds that railroads could claim by
making their roadbeds serve as levees;
Georgia lent to railroad companies $5,-
733,000; and so the story goes.[31] It should
be remembered that these issues were
not total losses, for where they were not
delivered there could be no loss, and
where the railroad had been built the
state when forced to foreclose on defaulted bonds became the owner of the
road. Some of the states after the raids
had been made passed constitutional
amendments forbidding aid to private
companies.

Railroad rings used other means to
reap rich harvests, such as bribing legislatures to sell their railroad holdings for
practically nothing, as in South Carolina
and in Florida, or as in Georgia which
used the state-owned Western and Atlantic Railroad for political purposes, and
later leased it under circumstances of
great favoritism.   Speaking of railroad
legislation in Alabama, General James H.
Clanton said that in the statehouse "and
outside of it, bribes were offered and
accepted at noonday, and without hesitation or shame," and that the effect of
these dishonesties was "to drive the capital from the State, paralyze industry,

---

[27] Augusta *Weekly Chronicle & Sentinel,* July
20, 1870.

[28] Montgomery *Alabama State Journal,* December 18, 1869.

[29] *Railroad Gazette: A Journal of Transportation*
(Chicago), IV (1872), 87.

[30] Garner, *Reconstruction in Mississippi,* 289.

[31] *Weekly Columbus Enquirer,* July 25, 1871;
Augusta *Weekly Chronicle & Sentinel,* July 19,
1871; Somers, *Southern States since the War,* 82
ff.; Nordhoff, *Cotton States,* 30, 58; McGrane,
Foreign Bondholders and American State Debts,
294–95; Albert B. Moore, "Railroad Building in
Alabama during the Reconstruction Period," in
Journal of Southern History, I (1935), 421–34,
437–38.

demoralize labor, and force our best citizens to flee Alabama as a pestilence, seeking relief and repose in the wilds of the distant West."[32]

The legislatures which engaged in these corruptions, railroad and otherwise, were controlled by the Radicals, but Democratic Southerners also took advantage of openings, though they had fewer chances. Nathan Bedford Forrest became much involved in Alabama railroad scandals but he was honest enough to impoverish himself in his efforts to recompense his creditors. Alabama Radicals sought to excuse themselves of their villainies by claiming correctly that the idea of state aid was "of Democratic origin."[33] Speaking of a state-aid bill before the legislature in 1869, a Radical charged that many "of its strongest lobbyists and largest beneficiaries" were "rampant, reactionary Democrats." They added, "Yet these very men, who expect to make money out of it, will use the argument that the Republican party had a majority in the Legislature, and will falsely, but hopefully, charge it upon Republicans as a partisan crime against the state." Democratic Southerners were forced to buy desired legislation other than for railroads — even for securing a charter for a college. And there were Democratic officeholders who partook of the same financial characteristics as Radicals. A Democratic official in Montgomery County, Alabama, defalcated to the extent of $50,000; in 1866 the Democratic treasurer of Mississippi stole from

that state $61,962; and the whole administration of Governor Robert Lindsay of Alabama (1870–1872) in lack of honesty differed little from the administrations of the Radicals between whom it was sandwiched.[34] In Georgia a Democratic editor emboldened himself sufficiently to make this charge: "It is a mortifying fact that the extravagance of Bullock's administration — we say nothing as to the corruption — benefitted about as many Democrats as Republicans."[35] It might also be added that Southern Democrats participated in the Salary Grab of 1873.

Through chartering the Louisiana Lottery in 1868 the Radicals set up an institution of such malodorous reputation that Alexander K. McClure could say it was "lavish in its gifts, ostentatious in its charities, and generous in public enterprise, but the Church could as well draw its financial sustenance from the bawdyhouse or the gambler's den, and hope to promote vital piety, as can the politics, charity, or enterprise of New Orleans draw tribute with self-respect from the lottery swindle."[36] Although this lottery had been chartered by a Radical legislature, it was owned and operated by

---

[32] *Weekly Columbus Enquirer*, March 15, 1870. Governor Warmoth of Louisiana considered corruption a normal condition in his state. "Why, damn it," he remarked, "everybody is demoralizing down here. Corruption is the fashion." Quoted in Shugg, *Origins of Class Struggle in Louisiana*, 227.

[33] Montgomery *Alabama State Journal*, December 18, 1869; March 25, 1870.

[34] Nordhoff, *Cotton States*, 74, 75, 90; Montgomery *Weekly Advertiser*, January 6, 1875; James D. Lynch, *Kemper County Vindicated, and a Peep at Radical Rule* (New York, 1879), 19; Somers, *Southern States since the War*, 132; Fleming, *Civil War and Reconstruction in Alabama*, 616, 740, 753 ff. The Montgomery *Alabama State Journal*, December 27, 1872, charged against the Democrats that "our common school fund has been squandered, and education languishes throughout the state; our lands are without a market; our warrents are being hawked about the streets, and can be sold only at a ruinous discount; our officers are unpaid; our treasury is empty, and our state is on the verge of bankruptcy."

[35] Augusta *Weekly Chronicle & Sentinel*, quoted in Elberton *Gazette*, July 4, 1877.

[36] Alexander K. McClure, *The South: Its Industrial, Financial, and Political Condition* (Philadelphia, 1886), 135.

Southerners and its periodic drawings were presided over by the Confederate heroes, Pierre G. T. Beauregard and Jubal A. Early. This evil institution stirred up such hatred throughout the country that it led people to believe lotteries were exclusive Radical inventions.

Lotteries had been chartered widely over the United States in early days, but they had been generally outlawed before the outbreak of the Civil War. Immediately afterwards they returned to the South and were chartered by the Johnson governments and by the Democrats after Radical rule was ousted. Lotteries always announced that they had been set up for a laudable purpose, however much the private gain might be. South Carolina organized one to promote immigration; lotteries for the distribution of land were set up in Georgia and Kentucky; Alabama chartered the Tuscaloosa Scientific and Art Association which offered prizes for the best essay on science, for the most useful invention in mechanics, and for the best work of art; the Mississippi Educational and Manufacturing Aid Society lottery paid the state $5,000 for the benefit of the University; there was a National Charity Lottery in Hot Springs; the Monumental Association conducted a $500,000 lottery in Georgia to erect a Confederate monument; and the ladies of Columbus, Georgia, set up a lottery to aid Jefferson Davis.[37]

Radical Reconstruction ruined the financial credit of the South and de-

pressed its securities,[38] though it is possibly true that one of the reasons underlying it was to produce the opposite effect, to enhance Northern investments in the South. The increase of state debts became fantastic. Records were so carelessly kept and maliciously destroyed that restored Democratic governments were never able to determine exact amounts, and many later commentators have been unscientific in their appraisals. South Carolina's debt has been estimated from $15,700,000 to $29,100,000; North Carolina's and Alabama's as high as $30,000,000; and Louisiana's at $50,-597,000, one fourth for the benefit of the state and the rest "squandered, or done worse with." Many bond issues were sold at a small fraction of their face value. Confusion has arisen because writers have not indicated what part of the debts was secured by railroads and other valuable property and the part that represented values evaporated and gone forever. The amount of debts piled up by local divisions, such as counties and cities, is past finding out, with many records gone and others widely scattered. Irrespective of amounts, it cannot be doubted that the South underwent fearful financial punishment under Radical rule.[39]

Another source of money, either to spend or to steal, was taxation. Since

[37] Natchez *Democrat,* August 15, 1867; Little Rock *Weekly Arkansas Gazette,* February 14, 1876; Montgomery *Weekly Advertiser,* June 23, 1868, April 27, 1869; Atlanta *Christian Index,* February 28, 1867; Rome *Weekly Courier,* March 18, 1874; Greenville *Enterprise,* June 7, 1871; Elberton *Gazette,* March 2, 1870; Augusta *Weekly Chronicle & Sentinel,* July 5, 1871; January 31, 1872.

[38] *The Commercial and Financial Chronicle* (New York), IV–VII (1867–1868), *passim; De Bow's Review,* IV (1867), 154.

[39] Nordhoff, *Cotton States,* 29, 57, 95; Coulter, *William G. Brownlow,* 375–77; Fleming, *Civil War and Reconstruction in Alabama,* 571–86; Davis, *Civil War and Reconstruction in Florida,* 679; Simkins and Woody, *South Carolina during Reconstruction,* 45, 148–85; Beale, "On Rewriting Reconstruction History," *loc. cit.,* 816. Vicksburg's debt rose from $13,000 in 1869 to $1,-400,000 in 1874. Garner, *Reconstruction in Mississippi,* 328 ff.

taxing is used more than bond issuing for the ordinary expenses of government, it was to be expected that taxes should be higher after the Civil War than before. This is so on account of the many additional services governments undertook to perform for the people. Education was now provided free for all people; more institutions such as insane asylums and poorhouses were set up; and the cost of administering justice was vastly increased. Formerly, if a slave committed a serious crime he received thirty-nine lashes, at no expense to the planter or the state; now, when Negroes committed crimes their arrest, trial, and punishment brought on expenses which the state must pay.

In ante-bellum times Southerners had never been subjected to burdensome taxes, and little of their revenue had been secured from land. In South Carolina in 1859 all agricultural lands were assessed for taxation at slightly more than $10,000,000, whereas lots and buildings in Charleston alone were listed at $22,000,000. With the coming of the Radicals, land was made to bear a greatly increased amount of the tax burden — and not on account of the ease in levying the tax or by simple accident. It was by special design, for those who set the taxes had little land, or, indeed, little property of any sort; but, as they wanted land, they saw that high taxes would depress its value and probably lead to its confiscation by the state for unpaid taxes. Here the Negroes and poor whites would find an easy road to landownership. Joseph H. Rainey, a South Carolina colored Congressman, said, "Land in South Carolina is cheap. We like to put on the taxes, so as to make it cheap!"[40] The

amount of land advertised for taxes increased with the carrying out of this program, until whole sections of some states were for sale. In Mississippi about a fifth of the state was advertised for taxes; in St. Landry Parish, Louisiana, there were 821 sales of land for taxes from 1871 to 1873; in Arkansas a book of 228 pages, reprinted from an advertisement taking up sixteen sheets in a large-sized newspaper and costing for one insertion $12,312, was required to list the delinquent lands there.[41]

In some places the tax rate, state, county, and city, ran as high as 50 mills, equivalent to 5 per cent of the assessed value of the property. Though property values in the eleven states which had composed the Confederacy were in 1870 less than one half what they were in 1860, the amount of taxes paid was more than four times the total in 1860. A South Carolinian who had paid a tax of fifty cents on his lands before the war, now paid $15; another complained that he was forced to sell his last cow to provide money for his taxes. And one of the most discouraging features of Radical taxes was that much of the money was stolen by the collectors. More than a half million dollars of taxes collected in 1872 in Florida were never turned into the treasury.[42] This situation led outraged landholders in many sections of the South to call taxpayers' conventions, one in Louisiana adopting the name of the Tax Resisting Association, which begged its tormentors for relief and sought more

---

[40] New Orleans *Weekly Times*, June 6, 1874.

[41] Raymond *Hinds County Gazette*, June 7, 1867; August 17, 1870; December 27, 1871; Little Rock *Weekly Arkansas Gazette*, January 16, 1872.

[42] *Compendium of the Ninth Census, 1870* (Washington, 1872), 640; *Compendium of the Tenth Census, 1880*, II, 1509; *Ku Klux Conspiracy*, I, 439.

practical methods of obtaining it. When Negroes secured land they began to take the white man's point of view on high taxes. The worst tax atrocities came in the South after 1870, but even with its highest taxes it paid little higher rates than were levied in some of the Northern states. In 1870 Illinois had a rate of 45 mills, when the average for the eleven former Confederate States at that time was only 15 mills. The poverty of the South as compared with the North is strikingly shown in this fact: in 1870 the state of New York with a rate of 24.6 mills collected $48,550,000, whereas the whole former Confederate States collected only $32,227,529, state, county, and municipal.[43]

Assuredly, then, Radical government had not given the South that protection of property promised in the first Military Reconstruction Act; did it do any better in protecting life? In a war-ridden region like the South there was destined to be violence irrespective of the efforts of governing authorities to prevent it — whether they be Johnson Conservatives or Grant Radicals. After the Radicals took hold, violence instead of subsiding increased, and for reasons not foreign to provocative actions by the new rulers. Negro militia, which were organized in many of the states, incited violence as much as they promoted law and order; Loyal Leagues incited Negroes into incendiarism and racial clashes. Pistol toting became a custom, and it was said that Colt's arms factory was kept busy supplying the Southern trade. Former Governor Perry of South Carolina wrote the Radical Governor Robert K. Scott, "Every week and every day we hear of houses, barns, gin-houses and stores being destroyed and robbed by the midnight in-

cendiary."[44] In one issue of an Upper South Carolina newspaper appeared rewards for the burners of the stables of eight different men, and the machine shop of another. "There seems to be no limit to the insolence of the Carolina negroes," declared a Georgia editor. "They have been taught to regard the whites as their enemies and, having the power, let pass no opportunity to inflict annoyance or insult."[45]

Called into existence by violence, the Ku Klux Klan added to it; riots of serious proportions broke out widely over the South, some provoked by the Klan and others not. Rufus B. Bullock, Radical governor of Georgia, admitted that crimes against Negroes increased from an average of seventeen a month before his administration to forty-six after he took hold.[46] One issue of a state paper carried proclamations of the Governor offering rewards of $15,000 or more for lawbreakers.[47] Early in his administration, 300 armed Negroes "led on by the vermin, black and white, native and imported," incited a riot by attempting to enter Camilla. It was estimated that 150 people were killed at various times in Jackson County, Florida, alone; and Negroes started the most serious riot in Alabama's history when at Eufaula they tried to prevent a member of their race from voting the Democratic ticket. Negroes in Vicksburg provoked a race riot in which a hundred former Federal soldiers and other whites took part, and in which

[43] *Ku Klux Conspiracy,* I, 228–29.

[44] Greenville *Enterprise,* April 12, 1871; April 3, 1872.

[45] Augusta *Weekly Chronicle & Sentinel,* January 7, 1874.

[46] Thompson, *Reconstruction in Georgia,* 257. W. H. McWhorter, Greensboro, Ga., to Sumner, May 14, 1869, in Sumner Papers, Box 92, No. 176; Tunis G. Campbell, Atlanta, to Sumner, April 19, 1869, *ibid.,* Box 94, No. 45.

[47] Marietta *Journal,* February 10, 1871.

three dozen Negroes were killed. In Louisiana under its miserable travesty on government there was no end of riots and lesser violence — the Colfax riot in which fifty-nine Negroes and two whites were killed, the Coushatta violence in which five Radical officeholders were murdered, and the famous New Orleans uprising of 1874 which was not unlike a Parisian revolution. So bad were conditions that General Sheridan who was sent to preserve law and order, to the amazement of sane people everywhere, asked for permission to declare banditti those Louisianians whom he cared to dispose of without further ado. In North Carolina a unique band of lawbreakers known as the Lowrie Gang seem to have suffered little hindrance probably because of their Radical leanings.[48]

Though it might appear that Radicals would be discredited by arguing violence in the South under their own rule, yet they did so with a great show of statistics to prove it. Their purpose was to induce the Federal government to send in troops to uphold their tottering régimes, or to "wave the bloody shirt" in the North to influence elections there. Governor Warmoth asserted that 3,000 Democrats killed 200 Radicals in the St. Landry riot in 1868; and for the Congressional elections of 1874 Representative Joseph R. Hawley of Connecticut got a list of Alabama atrocities from Charles Hays, an Alabama Radical Representative, which he used to great effect until the New York *Tribune* proved them to be myths. A meeting of Radicals from nearly all the Southern states came to-

gether this same year in Chattanooga to compile a stunning list of atrocities for the same election campaign.[49] Lucius Q. C. Lamar, Democratic Representative from Mississippi, asked these embarrassing questions: "When you point me to acts of violence, I acknowledge and deplore them; but I ask you, who has governed the States where this violence occurs, for the last ten years? Have we? Who have taxed us, controlled our legislatures, filled our courts, received the patronage of the Federal Government, ruled over us at home, and represented us here?"[50]

Radical Reconstruction had failed in every particular in which the Radical Congress had accused the Johnson governments. Radical rule in Louisiana had produced effects "which in ten years have sunk this fertile and once prosperous State into a condition of decay which it has taken Turkish misgovernment some centuries to bring about in the East."[51] And the people of New Orleans were described by a Northern traveler: "Ah! these faces, these faces; — expressing deeper pain, profounder discontent than were caused by the iron fate of the few years of the war! One sees them everywhere; on the street, at the theatre, in the *salon,* in the cars; and pauses for a

---

[48] Rhodes, *History of the United States,* VII, 112–22; Nordhoff, *Cotton States,* 48, 54, 79; James J. Farris, "The Lowrie Gang — An Episode in the History of Robeson County, N. C., 1864–1874," in Trinity College Historical Society *Papers* (Durham, 1897–), Ser. XV (1925), 55–93.

[49] Henry C. Warmoth, *War, Politics and Reconstruction: Stormy Days in Louisiana* (New York, 1930), 67. See also, Montgomery *Weekly Advertiser,* January 20, 1875; Macon *American Union,* September 25, 1868; Columbus (Miss.) *Press,* September 26, October 13, 17, 24, 1874; Nordhoff, *Cotton States,* 18. Henry B. Denman, New Orleans, wrote Zachariah Chandler from New Orleans, March 11, 1872, that four fifths of the whites there "hate the National Government with a bitterness that can hardly be realized and not possibly expressed or described." Zachariah Chandler Papers, V, Nos. 1072–73.

[50] Edwin A. Alderman *et al.* (eds.), *Library of Southern Literature* (New Orleans, Atlanta, Dallas, 1907–1923), VII, 2973.

[51] *Southern Magazine,* XVI (1875), 430.

moment, struck with the expression of entire despair — of complete helplessness, which has possessed their features."[52] Alluding to the New Orleans uprising of 1874, the *Nation* said there was no instance in modern times "in which the insurgents had more plainly the right on their side," and when the Federal troops were sent to put it down, this journal declared that the Austrians in their seventy years of tyranny in Italy had never "marched on so bad and despicable an errand."[53] An observer saw in Alabamians a despair "more dreadful and depressing than the negro ignorance."[54]

The more intelligent Negroes were beginning to see that their own fate lay buried with that of their Conservative white neighbors, and some of them began to avoid the Radicals and eschew politics entirely. Richard Harvey Cain, a Negro editor in Charleston, said, "When the smoke and fighting is over, the negroes have nothing gained and the whites have nothing left, while the jackals have all the booty."[55]

Also, it should not be assumed that there was no stern opposition and righteous indignation in the North against this Radical withering up of the South. The Democratic party platform in 1868 was strong in its denunciation, and Horatio Seymour, its candidate for President, condemned the barbarous rule of the Radicals. Frank Blair, the vice-presidential nominee, repenting that he had marched through Georgia with Sherman, threatened violence against Radical Reconstructionists. As for Federal com-

manders, Rosecrans, Sherman, George H. Thomas, George G. Meade, Winfield S. Hancock, George B. McClellan, Don Carlos Buell, Henry W. Slocum, John A. McClernand, William S. Franklin, and others either were silently ashamed or expressed their abhorrence of what was going on.[56] The editor of *Scribner's Monthly* saw Southerners in despair and he blamed the Federal government: "They feel that they were wronged, that they have no future, that they cannot protect themselves, and that nothing but death or voluntary exile will give them relief."[57] The editor of the *Nation* by 1870 had come to view the South with a light different from that of 1865. In the South the people had almost forgotten "that in free countries men live for more objects than the simple one of keeping robbers' hands off the earnings of the citizen."[58] There people were worse off than they were in any South American republic; for in the latter place tyrants could be turned out through the right of revolution, but the South with the army on its back could no longer resort to this ancient remedy. Southerners must continue to suffer enormities "which the Czar would not venture toward Poland, or the British Empire toward the Sautals of the Indian jungle."[59] The North with

[52] King, *Great South*, 34.

[53] *Nation*, XIX (1874), 199.

[54] King, *Great South*, 333.

[55] Charleston *Missionary Record*, quoted in Augusta *Weekly Chronicle & Sentinel*, November 22, 1871.

[56] Randall, *Civil War and Reconstruction*, 797–98.

[57] *Scribner's Monthly*, VIII (1874), 368.

[58] *Nation*, XIX (1874), 132. South Carolina had produced "not one, but a swarm of little Tweeds and little Butlers, some white and some black." *Ibid.*, XVIII (1874), 247.

[59] *Ibid.*, 326. "They are 'ex-rebels,' but they are not thieves. They have owned slaves, and revolted in defense of slavery; but they are influential, economical, and trustworthy in the management of State affairs, and it was of the first importance not only to the negro, but to the whole Union, that, during the transitional or reconstruc-

all its charities to the South had done less good than the Carpetbaggers had done harm.[60] Schurz had learned much since his first visit to the South in 1865. He saw fearful acts perpetrated against the South, all in the name of patriotism, and particularly in Louisiana, "a usurpation such as this country has never seen, and probably no citizen of the United States has ever dreamed of."[61]

---

tive period following the war, they should neither be driven into hostility to the local government nor prevented from giving it the benefit of their experience and ability." *Ibid.*, XII (1871), 212.

[60] Said the *Nation*, XIV (1872), 197: "Seven years have gone over us since the close of the war, and, instead of occupying this precious season with endeavors to re-establish prosperity and to sow the seeds of peace which, in another generation, would ripen into good-will and forgetfulness, we have averted our eyes from the whole problem, refused to listen to the complaints of men whose hands we have tied, and have fallen back upon the lazy belief that in some way this great country is bound to go through."

[61] King, *Great South*, 93.

Suggestions for Additional Reading

Among the general accounts of Reconstruction, several of the works of older historians are still useful, particularly for political aspects. Such works as James Ford Rhodes, *The History of the United States from the Compromise of 1850* (New York, 1906), vols. V, VI, VII; John W. Burgess, *Reconstruction and the Constitution* (New York, 1902); William A. Dunning, *Reconstruction, Political and Economic* (New York, 1907); Walter Fleming, *The Sequel of Appomattox* (New Haven, 1919), contain chapters on the southern states during the Reconstruction period. A comprehensive collection of source materials may be found in Walter L. Fleming's *Documentary History of Reconstruction* (2 vols., Cleveland, 1906–1907). Also of interest for this earlier period of historical writing is a series of articles on Reconstruction which appeared in the *Atlantic Monthly,* vols. 87 and 88 (1901). These included the following: Hilary A. Herbert, "The Conditions of the Reconstruction Problem"; William E. B. Du Bois, "The Freedmen's Bureau"; Daniel H. Chamberlain, "Reconstruction in South Carolina"; William Garrott Brown, "The Ku Klux Movement"; Albert Phelps, "New Orleans and Reconstruction"; Thomas Nelson Page, "The Southern People during Reconstruction"; William A. Dunning, "The Undoing of Reconstruction." More recent works which provide a general treatment are Claude G. Bowers' partisan study, *The Tragic Era* (Boston, 1929), and Robert S. Henry's *The Story of Reconstruction* (Indianapolis, 1938). The student will gain an additional understanding of the forces at work in southern life at the end of the Reconstruction period from Paul H. Buck's *The Road to Reunion, 1865–1907* (Boston, 1937), and C. Venn Woodward's *Reunion and Reaction* (New York, 1951).

Studies of particular states during Reconstruction are numerous, but the serious student will find many necessary details of political history in such books as: John S. Reynolds, *Reconstruction in South Carolina, 1865–1877* (Columbia, 1905); J. G. de Roulhac Hamilton, *Reconstruction in North Carolina* (New York, 1914); William W. Davis, *Civil War and Reconstruction in Florida* (New York, 1913); Hamilton J. Eckenrode, *The Political History of Virginia during Reconstruction* (Baltimore, 1904); Edwin C. Wooley, *The Reconstruction of Georgia* (New York, 1901); Thomas S. Staples, *Reconstruction in Arkansas* (New York, 1923); John R. Ficklin, *History of Reconstruction in Louisiana through 1868* (Baltimore, 1910); Charles M. Ramsdell, *Reconstruction in Texas* (New York, 1910). Even more useful because they include social and economic as well as political history are: James W. Garner, *Reconstruction in Mississippi* (New York, 1901); C. Mildred Thompson, *Reconstruction in Georgia, Economic and Political, 1865–1872* (New York, 1915); Francis B. Simkins and Robert H. Woody, *South Carolina during Reconstruction* (Chapel Hill, 1932).

There are many journal articles on special aspects of Reconstruction which give valuable insights into the effects of Reconstruction in southern social and political life. Among these are: Francis B. Simkins, "The Ku Klux Klan in South Carolina, 1868–1871," *Journal of Negro History*, XII (October, 1927), pp. 606–647; William B. Hesseltine, "Economic Factors in the Abandonment of Reconstruction," *Mississippi Valley Historical Review*, XXII (September, 1935), pp. 191–210; William E. B. Du Bois, "Reconstruction and Its Benefits," *American Historical Review*, XV (July, 1910), pp. 781–799; David H. Donald, "The Scalawag in Mississippi Reconstruction," *Journal of Southern History*, X (November, 1944), pp. 447–460; T. Harry Williams, "The Louisiana Unification Movement of 1873," *Journal of Southern History*, XI (August, 1945), pp. 349–369. In addition, no student who wishes to understand fully the many issues involved in Reconstruction as a historical problem should overlook three notable articles on the historians of Reconstruction: Howard K. Beale, "On Rewriting Reconstruction History," *American Historical Review*, XLV (July, 1940), pp. 807–827; Alrutheus A. Taylor, "Historians of Reconstruction," *Journal of Negro History*, XXIII (January, 1938), pp. 16–34; T. Harry Williams, "An Analysis of Some Reconstruction Attitudes," *Journal of Southern History*, XII (November, 1946), pp. 469–486.

DATE DUE

APR 13 1994			
APR 1 9 1995			

HIGHSMITH 45-220

WITHDRAWN